To Mike

my best regards

9/97

Great Book

MUST READ FOR

The whole family

MFD

9/97

The Road to Optimism

Change Your Language—Change Your Life!

Library of Congress Cataloging-in-Publication Data

J. Mitchell Perry with Richard E. Griggs
The road to optimism: change your language, change your life / J. Mitchell Perry.
      p.   cm.
    ISBN 0-922530-02-5:
      1. Change (Psychology). 2. Optimism. 3. Self-actualization (Psychology) . 4. Mind and body. I. Title.
BF637.C4P48   1996
158' . —dc20   96-33893 CIP

Edited by Fred Norman
Printed in the United States of America by Thomson-Shore, Inc.
Published by Manfit Press, San Ramon, California.

10 9 8 7 6 5 4 3 2 1

You may order this book from your bookstore. This title may also be purchased from the publisher in quantity discounts for your department or team.

Dedication

To my mentor, George Smainis, who taught me more than he could ever know about life. Because of his optimism and his gifts of power and beauty in the forces of nature, I am a better person.

Acknowledgments

Much appreciation goes to the staff of JM Perry Corporation for their assistance, support, and patience during the years it took to produce this book. You are wonderful—Kande Benson, Robert Fisher, M.D., Marty Friedman, Henry Lee, Sandy Poff, Steve Vislisel, Jerry Vorpahl, and Paul Wright. We also want to acknowledge Natalie Reed for her assistance with various stages of manuscript preparation. Special recognition is deserved by those who provided pivotal feedback on early and final drafts—Antonia Boyle, Margaret Lucke, and Fred Norman; you helped produce a quality product.

Contents

Preface

"This won't hurt" is a lie. It always has been and always will be. As soon as these words are spoken a sensation comes to mind—pain. The way we label events in our lives makes all the difference in the world. Why do doctors swear that the patient with the best attitude and outlook will recover best? These three simple words—"This won't hurt"—instead of calming and reassuring the listener, causes him or her to start thinking about rocks, needles, sticks, fists, fingernails, and all the other objects that have caused pain in the past. The little contraction at the end of *won't* doesn't make up for the word *hurt*. Your brain will focus on the *hurt*, which equates to discomfort somewhere in your being.

Imagine yourself biting into a tart, yellow slice of ripe lemon and feeling the cool juice squirt onto your cheeks and around and under your tongue . . . Now that's your brain in action, based on words. You may need to go get a sip of water! *The Road To Optimism* starts here—with the power of words and their impact on your life. Rather than use *"This won't hurt,"* let me say, *"The trip will be pleasurable and fascinating."*

Something unique happens to many of us adults. We shift our perspective from good to bad, from optimistic to pessimistic, from what's *there* to what's *not there*. As a young adult, I took a five-week trip to Europe with my father and brother. We took motorbikes and traveled through England, across the English Channel, and up the Seine river in a forty-foot boat. We then cranked up the bikes and continued across France and into Italy. My expectations of the trip vividly outlined inspiring sights, exotic food, outstanding company, and sizzling adventures. We had our setbacks, but today my memory holds the images of the sights, food, family, and the breathtaking adventures. I got what I envisioned.

You too will get what you envision. This book will help you become aware of when you speak in a manner that points out the *absence* of something! This creates pessimism and slows your progress in personal aims and business pursuits. I have been taking inventory of all the ways we describe our experiences and interactions in terms of what's not there. In fact, I began doing this in 1976 when I was in private practice as a Marriage and Family Therapist. I was shocked by all the problems caused by low self-concept and low self-esteem. People phrased their situations in terms that did them little good.

I've always thought that the final frontier for personal and business growth is to take responsibility for your thoughts, your behavior, and your destiny. As a therapist, I wanted to help people change their behavior. In business, I see the same need. People yearn for a tool to change their attitude from negative to positive, from pessimistic to optimistic, from self-defeating to succeeding. I looked around for many years for such a tool, and I finally discovered it.

The Language Inclusion Process is that tool. After I finally became aware of it, I was embarrassed that I had missed something so obvious. This book will describe how the Language Inclusion Process can make dramatic changes in just about every dimension of your life.

If you want to improve your own motivation and optimism, and if you also want to help those around you, read this book—read it twice—for a wonderful path toward changing your language and changing your life. Years ago, I would have said, "It won't hurt." Today, I encourage you to begin your wonderful journey—the sights are astounding!

Dr. J. Mitchell Perry
Palo Alto, California
July 1996

The Word on Chapter

1

As we stand on the shoulders of those who have gone before, we see that optimism has been well-researched. Optimism is connected to attitude, health, and longevity. Now, we just need a trail to follow.

THE VALUE OF OPTIMISM

—

A colleague of mine ordered some products from a mail-order catalog. They were high-quality reading and correspondence aids for his office. He carefully selected personalized stationery and envelopes and a sharp-looking cherry wood holder for a special corner of his desk. After calculating the costs for the products, engraving, and tax, he sent the order off and began to anticipate delivery of the handsome pieces. After six or seven days had passed, he received a letter from the company. It said that there was a problem with his order

—he had omitted the postage and handling and owed $13.95. He became angry and stopped reading after that line and prepared to retrace his calculations. His initial suspicion was that they were trying to squeeze more money out of him and he'd better not let himself be taken. He thought of the letter he'd have to write, the delay in shipment, and maybe being put on hold while he pressed a series of buttons to speak to a real person at the company. He wished he hadn't ordered the darn things. He felt negative and pessimistic.

Later, when he read the rest of the letter, his attitude completely changed. The letter stated that despite the slight problem, they had shipped the product anyway. This got his attention. It went on to say that they trusted his judgment and hoped that after reviewing the attached figures, he would send the remaining money. They even included a postage-paid envelope. He was jolted by the company's positive and trusting action, especially when he compared it to his defensive response. Their approach made him want to send the money without even double-checking his figures. These were people he wanted to do business with again and again.

PIONEERS IN OPTIMISM

This chapter will introduce you to some of the pioneers in the area of optimism along with some of their surprising findings, particularly in three areas: longevity, health, and productivity and performance. The value of optimism, their studies show, is enormous. It affects so many dimensions of one's life. Optimism is a mental state that is very often associated with positive emotions, a positive outlook, love, care, joy, happiness, laughter, and looking on the up side of things. Optimism is a very powerful state of mind. It is so powerful that it can have a significant impact on your whole being. If you are optimistic you will live longer, have fewer illnesses, recover faster from illness, and be more resilient.

The key is learning how to become optimistic. My view is that there is a missing link between simply wanting to be more optimistic and actually exhibiting behaviors consistent with an optimistic attitude. We need a way to get a handle on this attitude and support it in our lives when we need it most. Instead of just changing your mind, which is very difficult, you change your language, which in turn changes your mindset to one of optimism. In subsequent chapters I will present a tool to help you do just that.

WHAT IS OPTIMISM?

The nation's premier researcher on optimism is Martin Seligman, Ph.D., who has studied optimism more than anybody in America. He has found that an optimistic state of mind seriously influences many dimensions of your life.

Seligman describes people as having an *explanatory* style, which is the way in which your mind attempts to explain reality. Some people have a pessimistic explanatory style; others have an optimistic explanatory style. Listen to how they sound:

Pessimists think that if something good happens to them, it's a fluke, it can't be trusted, it's likely to pass. They believe that they don't deserve good things. "This is too good to be true," pessimists say, "this can't possibly last, when is the other shoe going to fall, now is the time you have to worry, hold up—I'm enjoying myself too much, I shouldn't be enjoying myself, I shouldn't be getting paid for this—wait a second, where's the catch?" In short, pessimists discount good experiences.

When bad things happen to pessimists, though, they embrace those experiences. They say, "This is right on schedule, I knew it, with Murphy's law this is always what happens, this is how life is, it's a dog-eat-dog world, life is a board-certified pain in the neck and then you die, I just knew this was going to happen."

"WOW, I LIKE THIS"

Optimists, on the other hand, when good things happen, tend to say, "This is great, I enjoyed this, this is wonderful, this is right on schedule, let's do more of this, I hope this continues for a long time." Optimists also tend to discount bad news, saying, "This is a fluke, it's a chance, it's a nuisance, it's an inconvenience, this will pass quickly, there is something for me to learn here, I am just going to dust myself off and recover as quickly as possible." The optimist's approach is to explain away the bad stuff and embrace the good stuff.

An explanatory style, according to Dr. Seligman, is something that is learned, which means it can be changed. By learning a new style, you can change the way you think from pessimistic to optimistic. This is an extremely worthwhile goal for your professional life and your personal life.

This book introduces a process that uses your language, what you say to yourself and to others, to improve your optimism.

Here is the definition of the process:

The Language Inclusion Process (L.I.P.)

The Language Inclusion Process (L.I.P.) is the road to extraordinary personal and business performance—a mental state of optimism achieved by understanding the special impact words can have on your brain. Since what you *say* influences what you *feel,* which also influences what you *think*, then speaking about inclusion, what's there right in front of you, is a most powerful method for guaranteeing optimism and real output in your life.

You will read much more about the Language Inclusion Process later. For now, let's explore the value of optimism or an optimistic explanatory style.

WANT TO LIVE LONGER?

In this country there are more than 36,000 people who are 100 years old or older. These centenarians are being studied more and more. The subject of geriatrics continues to be a source of fascination with researchers, particularly since baby boomers, the largest demographic swell in the country, continue to advance in age. Many studies have tried to find clues as to why centenarians live so long. What common factors or qualities do they share?

While variables like their gender, geographic location, diet, life-style, and genetic predisposition can vary, one quality they often have in common is an optimistic state of mind. They tend to recover quickly from setbacks, to have a sense of mission, and to have a well-developed sense of humor. They are generally very happy people.

The conclusion very well may be that the more you are optimistic, the more likely you are to live a long life. One of the oldest people in the world is a French woman named Jeanne Calment, who has surpassed the 120-year mark. Although wheelchair-bound, she maintains a very optimistic state of mind. She has been quoted as saying ten years earlier, "It took me 110 years to get this old and to become famous. I certainly am going to enjoy it as long as I can." She also said, "I'm indefatigable. I take one day as it comes." This is a woman who clearly is optimistic, who is clearly enjoying a very long life.

Dr. Seligman and other researchers have shown that people who are depressed die sooner, and people who are pessimistic tend to have much shorter lives. As a result of the studies on longevity, it can be concluded that a positive state of mind has an enormously powerful impact on longevity. An optimistic explanatory style can contribute significantly to your living longer.

In the last two decades, more and more medical research has been done to show that a positive state of mind, combined with regular medical treatment, can significantly affect one's physical health. Researchers doing studies on the clinical effects of positive states of mind have learned that love, laughter, joy, and a person's spirit and commitment to live have a wholesale impact on their ability to recover from illnesses.

In his two insightful books, *Life After Life* and *Laugh After Laugh*, Raymond Moody, M.D., has shown that a person's positive emotions reduce high blood pressure because arterial relaxation improves blood flow. Positive emotions also counteract fear, anxiety, and depression, which are linked to physical illnesses.

Cancer specialist Dr. Carl Simonton, author of the book, *Getting Well,* has shown clinically that positive emotions have a significant impact on the reduction of cancerous tumors. When cancer patients are referred to Dr. Simonton's clinic in Pacific Palisades, California, both they and their family members check in. This enables the patients to receive medical treatment in an environment of complete support, care, love, and positivity. According to Dr. Simonton, there is continual clinical evidence to show a significant increase in recovery from cancer among these patients. He has proven that a positive environment, one filled with optimism and love and care, significantly aids their improvement.

At the Stanford School of Medicine, Dr. William Frye specialized in research on positive emotions, and in particular, laughter. In his work he has found that positive emotions aid probably all the major systems of the body. Laughter and positivity improve circulation and give heart muscles a strong workout. Laughter fills the lungs with oxygen-rich air, it clears respiratory passages, it stimulates helpful hormones, and it diminishes tension from the central nervous system. In addition, positive emotions stimulate the pituitary gland to produce endorphins, which are called the body's natural pain-killers and pleasure-enhancers. Positive emotions also release catecholamines, which may combat arthritis.

According to David Bressler, Ph.D., who has done an enormous amount of research on chronic pain, your mindset has a tremendous effect on how you deal with pain. He contends that you need to adjust your perspective on pain to one of being in control of suffering.

He has proven that when you shift from a pessimistic outlook to an optimistic one, then the severity of your suffering decreases and your ability to recover increases; translation: Your mind has a wholesale impact on the nature of your suffering.

SMILE NOW . . . LAUGH LATER

Smiling has a powerful impact on the physiological condition as well. Dr. Robert Zagone, from the University of Michigan, has shown through his research that the act of smiling creates a physiological change that makes you feel better by changing blood flow through the carotid arteries. Simply by smiling, you have a positive influence on the way you feel.

Often people with pessimistic explanatory styles will say, "You give me something to smile about and I will feel better," or "I will smile when you give me something to smile about." What optimists would say is, "Smiling is good. I will smile first, after which I will notice more things to smile about."

Roberto Assoliogli, M.D., founder of psychosynthesis, has suggested in his research that laughter and positive emotions stimulate the digestive organs, especially the liver, facilitating more oxygen to the blood cells.

Dr. Bernie Siegel, M.D., in his books has continually demonstrated that a positive state of mind and love and care have a significant impact on people recovering from illnesses.

People who go through crises in their lives often become emotionally upset. They frequently have increases in physiological problems as well. When you are upset, you might say, "I'm getting sick to my stomach." Very often people who have gastrointestinal problems will notice that those problems increase when they are stressed or upset.

In my private practice, I have noticed for many years that people have more physical disorders and illnesses when they are emotionally upset or feeling pessimistic. People who had chronic illnesses very often took very poor care of themselves, tended to have chronic gastrointestinal disorders, chronic headaches, skin disorders, and recurring physical illnesses. It's difficult to conclude for sure that their mental state caused all of their physical problems. I do, however, notice the close connection. I have concluded that an optimistic explanatory style will aid your physical condition significantly and help you recover far more quickly from illness and have far fewer sicknesses.

Dr. Norman Cousins, the famous former editor of the *Saturday Review* and a member of the UCLA School of Medicine faculty, wrote two well-known books: *The Anatomy of an Illness* and *The Healing Heart*. In *The Anatomy of an Illness*, which was made into a television movie, he incorporated positive emotions and laughter as part of his own treatment for a serious disease. In addition to receiving traditional medical care, he checked himself out of the hospital and into a hotel room in which he watched comedy movies on a regular basis as part of his treatment. Later, when he had heart problems, he changed his life-style by improving his diet and exercise program and continued to emphasize the value of positive emotions. He proved through his personal experiences that a positive series of emotions enhanced his ability to recover from his illnesses, including a serious heart condition.

Dr. Dean Ornish, in his work on cardiology, has clearly shown that heart disorders can be caused by changes in diet, exercise, and mental state. I suggest that an optimistic state of mind, and optimistic explanatory style, can significantly help in recovery from illness.

PRODUCTIVITY AND PERFORMANCE

People often claim that they work best under pressure. I have concluded from my observations over many years that people really don't work best under pressure. The pressure they are referring to simply means a certain amount of tension to get them going and to discontinue procrastinating. What I have noticed is that optimum performance comes when people are very much enjoying themselves, when they're being open, when they're learning something, and they're relatively relaxed. I imagine that you would agree that if you are having a great time, if you are really feeling positive and you are "in your zone," you are much more likely to perform at high levels.

People who are pessimistic and who tend to interpret good news with fear and nervousness tend to have lower performances. Most patients, clients, and seminar attendees agree that pessimism pulls performance down. When I ask them if a positive and optimistic state of mind has a serious impact on productivity and performance, they all say absolutely, "Yes." This information has been substantiated by the research done by Dr. Martin Seligman, described in his book, *Learned Optimism*. He gives clear evidence that while people with a pessimistic state of mind can have very strong levels of performance, the performance levels of people with an optimistic state of mind are significantly higher.

When you have a pessimistic state of mind, you very well may give up and feel defeated before you start.

Research done by Charles Garfield, Ph.D., author of the book, *Peak Performance*, teaches us that people who are peak performers generally are optimists. They have a clearly defined sense of mission. They are focused on what they do. They put a high premium on both their personal and professional lives, and they spend over two-thirds of their time doing what they really prefer.

There is overwhelming evidence to convince us that an optimistic state of mind has a wonderful impact on productivity and performance. That is definitely true for the participants in my performance training course, the Perry Performance Classic. This three-day program teaches the mental technology of optimum performance. People spend half the time in the classroom learning the mental skills and half the time on the golf course putting those skills to test. We have found that people frequently improve their golf performance significantly by changing the way in which they think from negative and anxious to positive and happy.

Now that we've seen the power and value of optimism, the question becomes: How on earth do I actually change my mental state from pessimism to optimism?

WHAT "SHOULD" I DO?

You may have heard yourself say, "I shouldn't be so critical. I shouldn't be so negative." You may have heard loved ones or colleagues or other associates tell you, "You should be more positive. You shouldn't be so negative. You ought to be a lot happier. You shouldn't take it so personally. You shouldn't be so hard on yourself. You shouldn't worry because there's no reason to worry." When you say such things to yourself or hear other people say them, *it's difficult to change your mind.* In fact, when others tell you not to be so hard on yourself or not to worry, the situation seems to get worse. You worry more, ruminate more, and assume more of a crisis-junky mentality.

One of the unwanted aspects of our world today is negativity. It is used to get attention and create headlines everywhere we turn. Our society is largely built on an adversarial system. Our communities rally around and express themselves in negative terms. Our families suffer isolation and loneliness that often turns negative.

Your brain remembers and records all of this information. You are often unaware of it, but like the accumulation of toxins in our food supply, it adds up.

The good news is that we can overcome these cynical and pessimistic attitudes. It's not easy. Just look around. We are geared to emphasize the down side. That's why I'm thrilled that you are going through this book. It can break the cycle and introduce new behaviors that can direct you to the up side. But how do you do it? How do you get your arms around adopting a positive mind-set? *Deciding* that it is important to do it is one thing; actually learning *how* to do it is another.

It sounds easy to change your mind at will, yet in practice it's very difficult. We are creatures of habit. We tend to do what's familiar. If we have been rehearsing a pessimistic state of mind for many years, it's hard simply to change our minds.

The question really is: What tools do you have at your disposal that can help you change your mind? In my opinion, the Language Inclusion Process is that tool. Employed on a regular basis, it will help you become much more positive, help you switch from a pessimistic explanatory style to an optimistic one. As a result, using it will enhance your longevity, your health, and your productivity and performance.

SUMMARY

My wish is that, like my colleague at the beginning of this chapter waiting for his catalog order, defensive with the letter he had received, opening his eyes and finally seeing the good stuff, you will progress to the point where you can recognize when you are being less than optimistic and can control your use of language to move you toward optimism. It is true that this mental state of optimism is associated with positive emotions. That is good to know and good to apply in your life. As you continue down this road, you will learn how powerful this state of optimism can be and just how to include it in your daily life.

SMOOTHING OUT THE BUMPS
POINTS TO REMEMBER/THINGS TO DO

1. Slow down and withhold judgment when tempted to be negative.

2. Calibrate your explanatory style to see if you are generally on the optimistic or the pessimistic side.

3. Optimism is connected with health.

4. Optimism is connected with long life.

5. Optimism is connected with productivity and high performance.

6. You can change your explanatory style from one of pessimism to one of optimism.

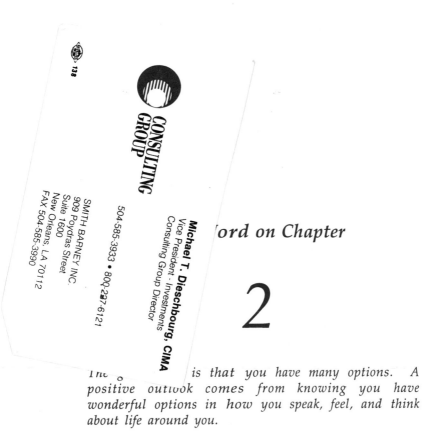

ord on Chapter

2

The *is that you have many options. A positive outlook comes from knowing you have wonderful options in how you speak, feel, and think about life around you.*

ILLUMINATE YOUR OPTIONS

—

"Life is a festival only to the wise."
Ralph Waldo Emerson

Now that you have given the value of optimism a big bear-hug, it's time to go to another area and do some illuminating. Optimism flourishes when there are ways out of a jam. In other words, when you have multiple choices, a situation is more manageable than it might seem. In fact, when you expand the paths open to you, you often feel a sense of control and direction in work and life. You feel as if you are in the driver's seat and can turn the wheel down whichever road you choose.

MULTIPLE OPTIONS

We have more choices than we think. We can choose different ways to drive to work or to the store. We can select from many items on most menus. Each of us can choose our profession, our hobbies, and our pursuits. Few of us, though, are truly proactive and genuinely make use of our choices. This is an area that is always a source of amazement for me because, although most people would agree that there are multiple options available to everyone in just about everything, only a select few make constant choices to pick from the broader menu of items in personal life and career work.

Adults most often think in two options. Polar options include right/wrong, good/bad, win/lose, all/nothing, success/failure. What's interesting is that when most people think in two options they tend to get very tense, they tend to get very rigid, and they tend to create conflict and/or stall decision making.

If you have a dilemma and I say to you, "Well, it sounds to me like you have only two options," how do you feel? You may respond identically to my clients and seminar audiences when I present this scenario to them—most report to me that they would feel backed into a corner and uncomfortable. However, if I say to you instead, "Well, it sounds like in your dilemma you have at least three options, perhaps more." Now, how do you feel? You'll notice that you feel quite different, because multiple options reduce mental tension and the *threat of the contest.* This creates space for your brain to relax and consider the flexibility you have to get yourself out of the dilemma or find the best solution. This mental tension or relaxation starts with the words you say to yourself. If you say to yourself that you are stuck in a bind, your brain re-encodes the message and works on it as if it were true. If you allow others to convince you that you have one way out and only one, you will begin to believe it. Your words to yourself can support or counteract that one-way thinking, which is quite prevalent wherever you turn.

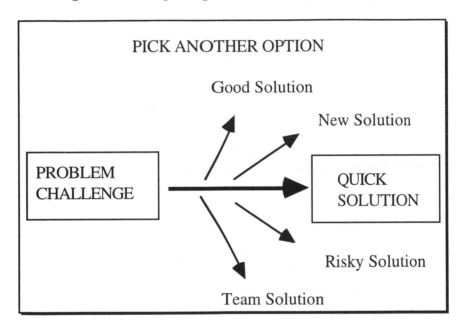

Finding multiple solutions requires thought and practice. It's often easy to find the first solution. The excitement and the press of time encourage you to get moving and do something. The best thing you can do is nothing. Nothing until you explore additional ways to resolve the issue or reach the objective. A point to remember is that, *your language influences your feelings, which influence your thoughts. By changing your language and speaking about the obvious, what's there—*

right in front of you—you guarantee optimism and real output in performance.

CUSTOMER SERVICE OPTIONS

Whenever I go around the United States and ask how many in the audience in Denver, Seattle, New York, Atlanta, Los Angeles, or Palm Springs are interested in having customers perceive their services to be of great value, having them pay the fee, and come back because the service value was greater than the fee, everyone says, "Yes," and agrees that this wonderful scenario depends on outstanding customer service.

Then I say, "Okay, let's change roles. Let's become buyers. We are going to buy a service or product, and we are going to pay a premium for it. We could be buying carpeting, or dental services, or legal services, or food, or anything. If we are going to pay a premium, how many of you think that outstanding customer service is required?" And everyone raises his or her hand. Then I say, "So whether we are buying the service or selling the service, outstanding customer service is absolutely essential," and everyone agrees.

Then I ask, "Okay, how many of you would say that whenever you get outstanding customer service from anyone, anywhere, it's usually a surprise and an exception?" Everyone laughs and a lot of hands go up.

So the question is: If it's so obvious that everyone demands outstanding customer service, why is it so rare? Well over three-quarters of all American businesses are service businesses, which means that in the grand majority of cases, the product is the service itself. Then why is it so rare to get outstanding customer service?

Part of the answer is that a supplier or seller may have jumped the gun and selected an option or service component that looked like it met customer needs but really failed to do so. It's often after the client or customer complains that additional options are quickly reviewed. The confused buyer goes away wondering why the supplier or seller failed to think it out better from the beginning.

You may wonder what this has to do with language and optimism. The key is that we get better results when we explore broader options. It helps us perform and makes us feel better. As we choose words to describe what we are feeling or experiencing, we find that some words make us think of narrow and constricting possibilities while other words make us envision broad and uplifting options. The interesting thing to note is that regardless which set of words we choose, the list of options is always there. Some people simply decide to resist listing them. It certainly seems reasonable, however, to pick words that help us focus on a bigger list to support us in meeting life's challenges.

CUSTOMER SATISFACTION OPTIONS

Very often I will ask chief executives, "How important is customer satisfaction? How important is it that your customers really are satisfied, and even better than that, delighted?" Everyone says, "Well, customer satisfaction is absolutely number one." And I say, "If customer satisfaction is number one, how are you doing with customer satisfaction?" And very often people will say, "Well, I'm not getting very many complaints, so I must be doing all right." I usually say, "Hold on. Wait a second. We all know that most people who are unsatisfied won't tell you—but they will tell a whole bunch of other people."

I then ask, "What kind of a systematic, ongoing, regular, formal and informal system do you have built into your business to actually determine levels of customer satisfaction?" The answer is usually vague and incomplete.

It seems practical and obvious that the best way to determine how well you're doing on customer service is to have a regular program to figure out from the customers themselves their level of satisfaction. A good way to get to this result is to keep pushing ahead for added solutions that will cover the largest area of concern for the longest period of time. *This is rarely the first solution that pops up at a team meeting or in a brainstorming session.*

THE MIND/BODY CONNECTION

Another area that's fascinating about illuminating your options is the mind/body connection. It is clear that the health of your mind affects your physical condition. Many physicians and psychologists will cite statistics about how 70-90% of all diseases are stress-related, mentally based, and life-style induced. This mind/body connection becomes clearer and clearer. We must ask ourselves how we feel about this linkage and whether we are doing anything about it. In the heat of the battle, can we take a break and go for a walk or get a glass of water? If not, what stops us? It would be difficult to stop us from taking the quick health break if we really believed that it would directly improve the critical task we are attempting to complete.

In his books, *Dr. Ornish's Program on Reversing Heart Disease* and *Eat More, Weigh Less*, Dean Ornish, M.D., has demonstrated that if you have heart problems and you dramatically change your diet to one with very low fat, and you dramatically change your exercise program to one of regular exercise, and you dramatically change your lifestyle to one of relaxation, and you consider the connection between the mind and the body, *then you are likely to achieve a significant reduction in heart disease and a significant increase in health.*

This seems evident, and yet very often we seem to require medical evidence to confirm what we know from common sense to be true—when you put a higher premium on your diet and your exercise and the mind/body connection, some very good things begin to occur. Both the mind and the body begin to significantly increase the way they work together for their mutual healthy benefit.

PHYSICAL CONDITION

In America, we are one of the richest countries in the world, but we squander our advantages so much that we spend our riches to counterbalance our excesses. We have access to the best technology; we have more food than anyone can eat; and we have a life-style that is unmatched on the planet. Our country provides all the resources we need to be in excellent physical condition in terms of both nutrition and exercise.

You may agree that, because of our excesses, we spend an enormous amount of energy and time and money on weight-loss products and physical conditioning equipment. While watching television, you will often see advertisements for diet aids and the latest exercise gear.

One in three people in America are obese. Two in three people are seriously overweight. In the last decade, the average American has gained approximately eleven pounds. If it's so obvious that physical condition is important (and it does seem obvious that we put plenty of money, time, and energy into physical conditioning), it is a mystery that many of us are in such terrible condition. Likewise, the best available information on nutrition says that people need a high-carbohydrate, low-fat, high-fiber diet strong in fruits and vegetables. Therefore, it is sad that people spend so much time eating nutritionally poor foods that are high in fat and cholesterol which contribute to heart disease, diabetes, and countless other forms of physical malfunctions. Exercise and good nutrition are closely connected to a person's well-being. If we overlook our eating and exercising there is something missing in our formula for happiness, health, and success.

JUST KEEP LOOKING . . . IT'S THERE

The dangers of smoking, alcohol, and drugs are hotly debated by those who pay the price and those whose jobs are supported by these industries. In particular, there is growing public awareness about the negative effects of smoking. As I mentioned earlier, it has been suggested by many different researchers that 70-90% of all physical ailments are life-style related, and the most destructive of all the life-style behaviors is smoking.

My aim throughout these chapters is to make the point that the obvious often plops itself right in front of us and we have trouble seeing it. Our next mistake is to polarize our options and eliminate all the good solutions that would emerge if we just kept looking. In this book, you will find that I am introducing a language-based process that helps us develop an attitude that keeps us looking in the right direction and in the right frame of mind. These language skills will apply to a few other areas. Let's take a look.

PERSONAL/PROFESSIONAL BALANCE

Another area in which the obvious is discounted or denied is the area of personal/professional balance. People's lives are dangerously out of balance while they deny the very thing that's important to them.

I frequently ask people in small and large group settings, "Between your personal life and your professional life, what one is more important to you in the long haul? Your professional life is whatever you do for a living, while your personal life consists of such elements as your personal health, your family, your marriage, your children, your spiritual life, your private time, and your friends." Resoundingly, well over 95% of the people I ask say that their personal life is more important. Then I ask, "How many of you are putting a premium on your personal life and attending to it, rather than to just your professional life?" Curiously, very few people raise their hands.

The paradox here is that though it's obvious that their personal life is more important to them, people spend more time in their professional life or doing something other than attending to what they say is important. My admonition to embrace those things that improve your life may sound too trite or simplistic. You may think you already do the right and logical thing most of the time. That's good. However, I want you to take another look.

My experience tells me that we often overlook what others can easily see in our lives. My suggestion is to slow down and calibrate your attitude and always remember to leave the door open to pick better options once you recognize them.

OBVIOUSLY MARRIED

Marriage is another area that contains the paradox of the obvious. Very frequently I ask people, "For those of you who are married, I would imagine that the person to whom you are married is the person with whom you feel the greatest degree of investment, the greatest degree of vulnerability, the greatest degree of intimacy, the greatest degree of trust. This is the person you've committed yourself to, this is the person with whom you have taken vows, this is the person with whom you have invested time and energy and emotions and money and your life. How many of you say that is true?" Many of the people raise their hands. Then I say, "Certainly, then, that must be the person whom you want to treat with the most indifference and contempt!" And everyone laughs.

The point is that very often the person with whom you are the most invested and most vulnerable is also the person you treat with the greatest indifference and disrespect. Is it any wonder that so many marriages end up in divorce—fifty percent in this country—or are lacking in terms of their happiness? Most of the time it is very difficult to count many married couples that you truly think are very, very happy and really get a kick out of each other.

Many people who have been married a long time feel a tremendous degree of loneliness. They feel estranged, isolated, disconnected, unloved, uncared for, and detached from the person to whom they are married. Frequently they spend time criticizing their partner, defending themselves or spending their energy in disallowing the other person to get close. I've seen surveys that suggest what married couples really are looking for from each other is to be understood; therefore, the most obvious thing people need to do in marriages is spend more time being sensitive and more time listening to one another. However, I've found that sensitivity and listening are often the first things to go in most marriages.

The thing that really works, and the thing that is usually missing, is *listening*—most married couples spend very little time listening to each other; hence, they end up shut out, estranged, isolated, and unhappy. They're very lonely and desire to be with one another, yet they look for all kinds of distractions or reinforcement elsewhere rather than reaching out to one another and spending time listening to one another.

PARENTING

What is the most obvious is often what is the most discounted among parents.

When small children come up for cuddling, very often the parents will cuddle them and love them. When the five-year-old child says, "Mom, Dad, watch me. Look at me. Look at what I can do," most parents will say, "Good for you, well done." When I have asked parents, "Why do you say, 'Good for you, well done,'" they will say, "Well, I want to reinforce my children's actions or behaviors. I want to tell them that they are doing a good job so that they will do more." The obvious rule is that if you reinforce the desired behavior, you are going to see more of it.

Michael Leboeff, in his book, *The Greatest Management Principle*, presents an axiom that I think makes great sense—"What gets rewarded, gets done." In all parts of life, if you reward certain types of behavior on a regular basis, you are more likely to get more of that behavior.

What is surprising, though is that some parents do the opposite of what we discussed on the previous page. As children get older, these parents spend more time criticizing the bad behavior and ignoring the good behavior, though it is obvious that what gets rewarded, gets done.

Many children, particularly those who have gotten into trouble with the law or who are underachievers, come out of childhood with very low self-esteem. The primary contributing factor to low self-esteem is the fact that these children feel unloved, the good they do is unreinforced, and they feel abandoned by their parents; meaning, the very thing that children want is the obvious—love, care, and unconditional regard. The very thing parents give lip-service to is the very same thing parents very often withhold. Embracing the options would give parents a chance to see the folly of withholding something that is useful. My point is, first, to make you think about it and second, to provide some verbal tools (Language Inclusion Process) that will help you do it once you have increased your awareness.

MORE REINFORCEMENT . . . PLEASE

In working with countless businesses in over twelve different industries world-wide, I have learned that if there is one yearning that is universal, one thing that most employees really want more of from their management, it is reinforcement. People in business are starving for more reinforcement, more positive regard, more of being told that what they are doing is right.

Ken Blanchard, in his book, *The One Minute Manager*, says that one of the ideas that is essential in managing people is to catch them doing something right, to tell them what they are doing well. Most people will agree intellectually that if you tell people what they are doing right, they are probably going to do more of it. Unfortunately, this type of clear feedback is rare or poorly delivered, if at all. The very thing that works is the very thing that is done the least. Therefore, one of the most effective things that can be done is simply to increase the frequency of reinforcement, the frequency of care and regard, and then the severity of problems in many areas of your personal endeavors and in your business will certainly decrease.

THE STRONG ASK FOR HELP

Here is another of my questions and answers with an audience. I have asked thousands of people, "If I want to get your cooperation, if I want you to become engaged, if I want you to sign up, if I want you to participate, if I want you to be a part of the team, what is one of the most effective ways for me to get you to be part of the team?" The overwhelming response is always, "Ask me for my help."

The single most common thing that people say that gets them to engage is to be asked for help. Yet asking for help is too risky for some people, or it goes against an attitude of self-sufficiency that deludes many others. What's surprising is that when I ask you for help, your first impulse is to say, "Okay," yet most of us associate asking for help with weakness. *Ask yourself, are you weaker when you ask for help, or are you in fact stronger?* When you decide to associate asking for help with strength, it becomes easier and more reasonable to simply ask for what you need. It's obvious.

CAREER CHOICE

Too many people spend their lives doing a job they dislike. So often people will stay in a job simply because of security or because they've been doing it for seniority or because they're too frightened to do something else. If you are pursuing an objective that you really enjoy, that you really find exciting, that really consumes your thoughts, you probably are going to have all of your pistons firing and your results will be maximized.

Dr. Wayne Dyer, in his book, *The Sky is the Limit*, says, "Follow your bliss." Translated: If you spend most of your time concentrating on what really turns you on, you're going to do better.

Dr. Charles Garfield, in his book, *Peak Performance*, notes that many thousands of peak performers he has interviewed spend over two-thirds of their time doing what they really prefer. This means that the single biggest predictor of success is preference. If you move in a direction that is consistent with what your dreams compel you to do, what really turns you on and utilizes your skills and is a good fit with your disposition, chances are good that you will do very well.

You would have plenty of trouble wearing clothes that didn't fit well. It would be incomprehensible to wear a size that was too small, or way too big. However, some folks chose vocations that do not fit and find themselves stuck, thinking that is their only option.

INVESTMENTS/RETIREMENT

We all know that our lives are limited, that in later years we are going to have less earning power, and ultimately we will die. Yet many of us refuse to acknowledge the issue of retirement. Most people, according to surveys in *USA Today*, are seriously under-funded when it comes to setting up their retirement. Most people resist setting aside money for the future; they are under the illusion that somehow it will take care of itself.

People are living longer; it's obvious, then, that they are going to need money for retirement. A first solution is to regularly set aside a percentage of money in your earlier years to ensure a comfortable retirement in your later years. I would wager that after reading this chapter and the next you will be primed and able to add solutions to this retirement scenario and many others. Can you add options to the question of retirement savings? Take a few minutes to think about it, then tackle the next chapter. It will be interesting and obvious.

SUMMARY

You can put a beautiful smile on your face as you highlight the many options in the banquet of your work and personal life. That same smile looks good on others too! In other words, you have an impact on yourself and the people around you. When you illuminate *their* options, you add something to their lives. When you do this for yourself and others, you have taken a negative and unappetizing snack and turned it into a positive, open-ended feast. Let's eat!

SMOOTHING OUT THE BUMPS
POINTS TO REMEMBER/THINGS TO DO

1. The first option or solution usually comes easily.

2. Later options will probably be better and more complete solutions to the challenge.

3. You are at the wheel and can decide which roads to take as you engineer optimism into your life.

4. Adding options gives your brain a rest so you can be more relaxed and effective in solving your work and life issues.

5. Reinforcement is a key ingredient.

6. The closer people are in your life (spouse, kids, co-workers) the more you must do to see the obvious connections.

7. It takes time to generate multiple options.

8. Asking for help signifies strength, openness, and a healthy attitude of trust.

3

Thank you for starting something that can "make your day." As you read and study these pages you will learn about optimism in ways that can also improve your week, your work, and your life. Keep reading!

EMBRACE THE OBVIOUS

—

"With all the terrible things that happen, with all the terrible people, I'm still an optimist, I still believe in the goodness of people."
Terry Anderson, former-hostage in Lebanon

This book is about making choices that lead to an optimistic attitude. Your attitude can be learned and it is quite "contagious." With this book in your hands you have identified yourself as a learner. You are interested and open to new ideas—fresh ideas that will change the way you look at words and feelings and thoughts. My background in offering therapy to individuals and families and in giving managerial and executive consultations to businesses has shown me that all humans want to see improvement in their lives, in their relationships, and in their professional interests. Perhaps you have selected this book after some prompting by a friend or loved one. Maybe you found the cover interesting or saw a chapter title that piqued your interest. Whatever the case, you have acted—you initiated something by beginning an open-minded stroll down a trail that will challenge, confuse, and sometimes even mystify you. If you persist, and keep moving, I guarantee you will find useful insights for your personal life, your relationships, and your career interests. One of the first insights is how your words affect you. The Language Inclusion Process (L.I.P.) recognizes the power of the words you say to yourself and to others.

Your language influences your feelings, which influence your thoughts. By changing your language and speaking about what's there—right in front of you—you guarantee optimism and real output in performance.

This chapter will help to focus your vision on something that is so simple but largely overlooked. When we see things over and over, something strange begins to happen. Our brains discount the usual, perhaps in an effort to quickly identify the new and interesting. Or perhaps to spot danger before it gets too close. The result is that the things right in front of you move to the background of your consciousness. You may no longer notice a row of books on the bookshelf or several framed photos on the desk until someone changes one of the books or photos. This is fine in most cases. Your mind does a masterful job of bringing important things to your attention and putting the rest on auto-pilot so you can attend to current and important things, and these things are usually connected with your immediate survival, your current happiness, or simply today's activity list.

The risk is that we begin to form patterns and sink deeper and deeper into a rut. We do the same things over and over and expect our lives to somehow get better. We behave in the same manner toward other people in a relationship and expect the relationship to improve. We perform our work duties the same old way, yet feel we deserve to be promoted or to make large sales.

A good skill to develop is to learn to separate what you really should be consciously aware of and what you can safely leave in the background. This book is about sharpening your awareness so you can harness what is already there in front of you. The tools and ideas and methods are waiting for you. Take them and use them to better yourself, your relationships, and your life.

FIGURE—GROUND

Psychologists have categorized this sharpening of awareness as figure-ground theory. You may recall seeing in a high school or college class a diagram with hundreds of tiny dots. If you kept looking at the diagram you would suddenly begin to notice the outline of a person, an animal, or some type of structure. The object became the *figure* and the rest remained in the back*ground*. It is precisely this skill—separating figure from ground—that determines our level of confidence and competence as we move through this world. As we will see in the next chapter, this ability to separate the important from the unimportant adds to our options in our language choice, in how we feel, and in how we think.

WHERE IS THAT GLUE?

Sometimes we have difficulty seeing what is directly in front of us. Matthew, a middle-age professional living on the west coast of the United States, was repairing some items around his house. They included shelving, billiard cues, and a broken chair leg. After completing the sanding and preparation, he went into the garage to find the bottle of wood-repair glue. He didn't remember exactly where the bottle was, but he was certain he had seen it over the past two years on a shelf in the garage. He stared at the shelf but his eyes could not find the bottle of glue. He had read about the *figure-ground* phenomenon, and knew that since his eyes had seen it so many times in the same place, he probably just didn't *see* the bottle of glue. He remembered the times he looked all over for his wallet or sunglasses only to find them in his hand or on the table directly in front of him. Sometimes you can't see what's right there. Matthew looked to see that no one was watching, and then he turned his head sideways, squatted close to the ground, and blinked several times in order to give his eyes a different perspective—still no bottle of glue.

Later, he found the original bottle upstairs in a bathroom where he had seen it many times over the past several months. His antics in the garage didn't help him then, but he was surely on the right track. His bottle of glue had been sitting in an equally obvious place, invisible to his eyes yet directly in view. Much of our personal history and career progression has been impacted by what we might call the "lost glue bottle" syndrome. We miss out on opportunities because we just can't focus our eyes to embrace what is there.

A CURIOUS PARADOX

Having been in the business of psychology for over twenty years, I have been amazed at some of the very powerful puzzles or contradictions of the human condition. One of the most curious is what I call the paradox of the *obvious—That which is right in front of your face is almost impossible to see. That which is most obvious is the last thing you'll ever recognize. (And, the answers and the magic are found in the obvious.)*

More and more in my work as a consultant, trainer, diagnostician, and teacher, national and international companies are asking my firm to help people at the top levels to recognize the obvious. These people are often paying to diagnose and treat conditions that are so obvious that the only people who have trouble seeing the blatantly apparent facts are the people who hired us.

Whether it's in performance or athletics or public speaking or sales or international relations or parenting or marriage, most often the obvious is under-utilized and unrecognized. You may find yourself nervously searching for your missing glasses only to discover that they've been on your nose the entire time.

Seeing past the negative may be like a painting you might see in an art gallery—a dirty, broken, abandoned horse-cart before a beautiful landscape scene. There are dozens of optimistic landscape scenes obscured by negative and pessimistic thoughts. We humans have a nasty little habit of allowing upsetting events to take over the whole screen or canvas when they really don't deserve such power. When we allow ourselves to only see the *figure* of the worrisome event, we miss all the wonderful opportunities waiting in the background. These opportunities may be silent, but they are always there for the optimistic person who searches for the colors that make life a picnic and careers successful.

If you have read this far it means you are primed and ready to learn how to see the good stuff more often. Keep reading to uncover more tools and skills that expand your vision so you can see all the beautiful colors supporting and bathing that run-down cart on the canvas.

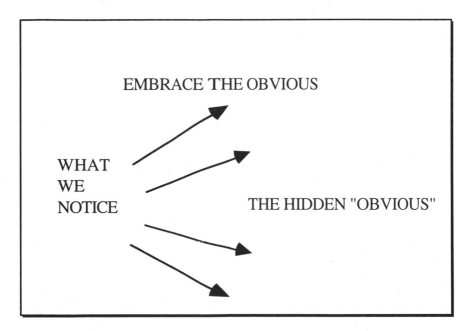

THE "HIDDEN" OBVIOUS ... BUT EMBRACED

This may test your powers of memory. Think back to your world history or your science classes. You may recall that some of the most amazing discoveries in history came about when someone took a different direction than everyone else around him or her and found a solution to a puzzle that afterwards seemed so obvious. Here's one that will test how hard you studied.

Max Planck, the German physicist, shocked the scientific world in the year 1900 with his outrageous idea that radiant energy (light waves) wasn't emitted in one solid flow but in small chunks. This was the starting point for the quantum theories that have revolutionized physics and helped us understand the nature of radiation. But how did "Herr Doktor" Planck get past the blind spot and see what no one else could envision? He risked being called a crackpot because his ideas were so different from what people believed at the turn of the century. He boldly said that light is really made up of exact units or multiples of a *constant* —a *quantum*. For the most part, Planck was right. His concepts were used by Albert Einstein (theory of relativity) and Niels Bohr (atomic structure), and, in 1918, he was awarded the Nobel Prize. Max Planck saw what was in front of him and risked talking about it.

AN *OBVIOUS* FOLK REMEDY

Here's another story about opening our eyes to the obvious. Edward Jenner, the English physician, developed and popularized the method for vaccinations against smallpox. This was a disease that killed up to 20% of those who got it and left another 15% permanently disfigured, and it struck children most often. There was a method of injecting weakened smallpox into healthy people, but it killed many of those inoculated. Jenner had heard from the farmers and dairymaids in his region that after contracting cowpox, people never got smallpox. He reasoned that since the cattle disease cowpox could be transmitted to humans without harm, this would be an obvious method of inoculation without the dire results of using real smallpox. He was right and is credited with wiping out the disease. Remember, it was an obvious common folk remedy that the medical profession of the time overlooked.

OPTIMISM/PESSIMISM

What is amazing about this is how the obvious is beaten, dragged, and hidden from our consciousness. In my consulting and seminar sessions, I ask people if most children are optimistic or pessimistic. The majority of my consulting clients and seminar attendees report that children are generally optimistic. Conversely, when I ask the same groups about adults age twenty-one and up, they say that most adults are pessimistic. We may be on to something! We'll add more to this later.

Take a look at how children speak. What do they say? What is their language? How does that differ from grown-ups and their choices of language patterns? The more you answer these questions, the more it's obvious that children speak in a language of inclusion and adults speak in a language of exclusion. The little children talk about what is there—the big kids speak about what is missing.

The next several chapters will dissect this curious connection between language and optimism. You are beginning a journey that can dramatically affect your life and all that you do.

WHICH IS MORE PRODUCTIVE?

Optimism or pessimism—which is more productive? Which has more influence on your performance? Which has more value? Which is preferable? In my two decades of providing therapy and consulting, most people when asked these questions say that optimism has more horsepower. If it does, why do most people opt for a pessimistic thought process over one of optimism?

WHAT IS OBVIOUS

There are many areas where research continues to pile up and conclusions seem cut-and-dried: Customers respond to good customer service; customer satisfaction is increased by personal attention; the mind and body are connected; personal and professional balance increase accomplishments; parental attention assists in child-rearing; exercise leads to better health, etc. If all of these areas appear to be so obvious, then why is it that we spend so much time discounting them?

My answer is that very often we will discount the obvious because we are looking for the complex as opposed to looking for what's right in front of our face.

This book is designed to help you steer in the direction of the obvious, to give you a specific skill you can use on a regular, comfortable basis, to ensure that you will be in control of your attitude. As a result, you will be in better control of many life areas important to you.

WHO SHOULD READ THIS?

The single most powerful indicator of becoming an adult is the willingness to take full responsibility for your behavior, for your destiny, for your feelings, for your thoughts. When people do take responsibility for their thoughts and their destiny, just about every dimension of their lives functions more fully. Yet many people and groups strenuously resist this idea. They prefer to call names, blame others, or claim victim status—in other words, to assign responsibility for their lives to someone else. If this is your determined method of survival, this book is better read by someone else. The information it contains is for those who dream of achieving a better awareness of the obvious and maximizing their options in life. If that's you, keep reading!

"YOU . . . ARE NOT A CROOK!"

A crook can spend exactly the same amount of time, energy, and ingenuity figuring out how to rob a bank as it might take him to legitimately earn the same amount of money he might steal. It takes energy to dwell on the negative. It takes energy to embrace productive options. Either road must be navigated and managed. It seems reasonable to select a direction that has better possibilities, offers longer benefits, and omits the crook's disguise!

Now, ask yourself a question: *If you were offered a way to make taking responsibility for yourself easier and less frightening, would you take it?* We all know the answer, don't we?

SUMMARY

So, like our friend Matthew trying to freshen his eyes so he could see the bottle of glue that he knew was there, this book will present some new ways of seeing the "good" stuff as you augment the options at your disposal. The next chapter will include three parts of your life that work together in some amazing ways. Now is the time to select the areas you can best control so that all three work toward your happiness, your effectiveness, and your ultimate satisfaction in life.

SMOOTHING OUT THE BUMPS
POINTS TO REMEMBER/THINGS TO DO

1. Your choices will impact your optimism.

2. It's often very difficult to see what is right in front of you.

3. Be aware of the figure-ground phenomenon and keep looking for the important options hidden by all that background stuff.

4. The complex is often a poorer solution.

5. Children start out optimistic and begin to lose it as they become adults who are more pessimistic.

6. Productive and non-productive activities and habits take equal time to develop and perfect.

7. Your language choices will have a powerful impact on future attitudes and actions.

8. Work on embracing the obvious.

The Word on Chapter

4

Sometimes we all wish to better control our feelings and thoughts. Here's a logical path to use your words in a way that affects what you feel and what you think.

THE BEHAVIOR TRIANGLE

—

"Our speech has its weaknesses and its defects like all the rest—most of the occasions for the troubles of the world are grammatical."
Michel de Montaigne

Here's an exciting section where you will learn more about the connection between what you say and its effect on your thoughts and feelings. Words, feelings, and thoughts—these three elements combine in unique ways to produce results in your life. They are like the ingredients used to make cookies. I enjoy making my special cookies for friends and family. Three of the ingredients are flour, sugar, and walnuts (the rest is secret). If I use too much flour, it will have an effect on the sugar and even the nuts. People will taste the difference (and sometimes give me strange looks). One ingredient always affects the others. This cause-effect relationship has intrigued marketers and product development engineers throughout industries that design products and services and then offer them to the world. They desperately want to find out what it is that produces the good or the bad outcome (effect). If they find it, it is as if they found the holy grail and everything became clear. The cause-effect question has haunted AIDS researchers and public health officials. Through the 1980s and 1990s, these researchers were first baffled and then buoyed as the cause-effect mystery of AIDS finally began to slowly unravel.

We all want to connect the pieces of the puzzle in each of our lives. We do things and wonder why. Our friends and family engage in certain behaviors (good and bad) and we scratch our heads and ask ourselves, "What in the world prompted them to do that?"

COOKIES . . . AND OPTIMISM?

When you consider the ingredients that create the outcomes in your life, it is reasonable to focus on those where you have the most impact, the most leverage, in order to achieve the best results. Among thoughts, feelings, and words, your best bet is to focus on the words.

Thoughts and feelings are hard to control, but you have total control in choosing your words. Yet, as we will see, your words help shape your thoughts and feelings, so when your words change, your thoughts and feelings will, too.

You can use the Language Inclusion Process to help you become more positive and optimistic by making gradual and permanent changes in your selection of words. It may seem too simple at this stage, but as you progress you will see the impact of words on your own thoughts and feelings and on the thoughts and feelings of those around you. People are attracted to optimistic people like iron is attracted to a magnet. This attraction to optimistic people seems quite natural and is often unconscious. You don't always know why, but you like that type of person. These people have something that others recognize and value. You can be this type of person as you continue devouring this chapter and the rest of the book. Whether you are reading this for personal or professional development, with the Language Inclusion Process, the "cookies" of your life will come out of the oven smelling and tasting great.

THREE POINTS FOR ATTITUDE

The Language Inclusion Process starts with a triangle. It gears us up to visualize the triad of elements that produce our success or failure. It is encouraging to know that any improvements you make in what you *say*, what you *feel*, and what you *think* will have a good payoff in the other areas of your personal and professional pursuits. The straightforward interrelation among these three ingredients suggests that the good you accomplish by working with them gets multiplied. Also remember that the bad, when it comes to these three, gets multiplied as well. This entire book will show, in some dramatic ways, how they depend upon each other. Here's how it looks in a diagram.

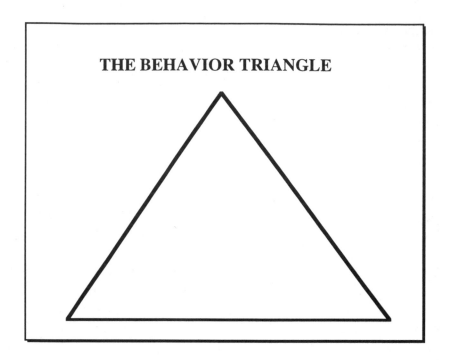

THE BEHAVIOR TRIANGLE

YOUR FIRST STEPS

Now add the words <u>say</u>, <u>feel</u>, and <u>think</u> to the diagram. Consider this: Since these three are so closely tied together, it is worth stopping here and absorbing the basic connection.   This is the foundation for the entire Language Inclusion Process.   In sports, music, and business, the basics are always a major key to progress and ultimate success.   In fact, it's hard to think of any endeavor where it's worth skipping the basics to rush into the details. This simple triangle will help you in the heat of the battle.   Bring it to mind when you are surrounded by people who enjoy wallowing in the negative and the cynical parts of life.   Bless their hearts, but notice how seductive negativity can be. Your future depends on understanding the causes that create your results. Optimism, based in reality, creates the best effects, and. this triangle will help you engineer that optimism.

Here are some additions to the diagram that show the relation between the three elements. You may find that in your own life two of the elements may be more closely tied together than the third. If that is true for you, pay extra attention to the two that seem closely linked. As you do this, continue to keep track of the third.

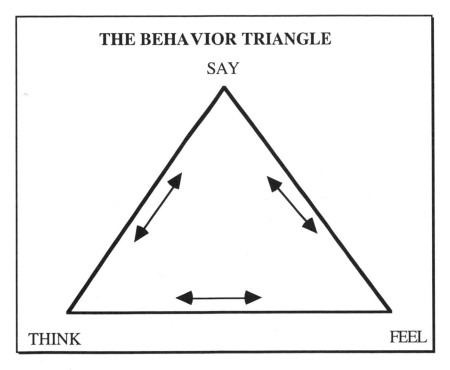

THE BEHAVIOR TRIANGLE

SAY

THINK   FEEL

The equation is: What you say affects how you feel. How you feel affects how you think. And vice versa. All language, feelings, and thoughts interact with each other forward, backward, every which way, and the entire accumulation of those influences creates your output and behavior. This is the complete behavior triangle. If you change one element—your language—your thoughts and feelings will be changed as well. The cumulative impact will be new patterns of output and behavior.

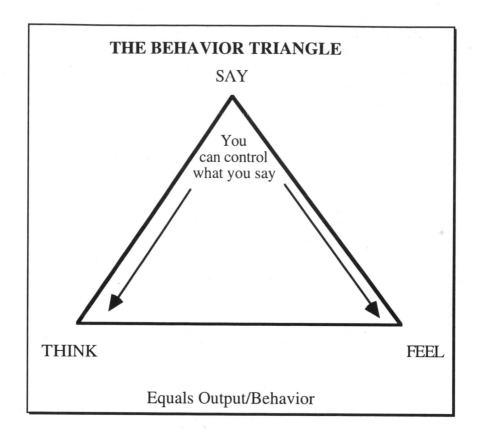

THE BEHAVIOR TRIANGLE

SAY

You can control what you say

THINK

FEEL

Equals Output/Behavior

HEY!... WATCH YOUR LANGUAGE

Suppose you want to control one of the three elements. You want to edit it, slow it up, start it, speed it up, stop it, amplify it, and change it in every which way. The language corner of the triangle is easier to control than the other two. This is where you can make a conscious decision to try something new.

Feelings are difficult to control because they sometimes consume our minds. In addition, feelings are often off limits, untouchables. Some feelings, such as hurt, sadness or anger, are so uncomfortable for people, they just refuse to feel them. To try to control them is often a gigantic challenge. There are some people who are referred to as being out of touch with their feelings. It is very challenging to control something that you have trouble identifying.

It is also a difficult job to control your thoughts. It's strange how thoughts come into your mind, and it is very difficult to get them out. There are times when you really want to quit thinking about something, but it just continues to haunt you and consume you.

PERISH THE THOUGHT ... PLEASE!

Sometimes your mind will dig up an image or thought you would rather forget. For example, many of you would like to be better at remembering names. You find that you have forgotten a person's name within the first few seconds after meeting them. After a class, book, or lecture on remembering names, you learn to associate something with the person's name. This will help you remember. Sam is a common name. It's so common it's easy to forget. Let's say you associate the name *Sam* with *Green Eggs & Ham* (the book by Dr. Seuss). You find that the association works—all too well. Every time you see Sam it's difficult to look him in the eye because your thoughts invariable go to . . . green eggs and ham!

There are other thoughts worth dwelling upon, but they're free-floating. We often need to direct concentrated thought toward a family member, paying our debts, or a critical career project. We want to have this thought in our mind, but competing thoughts keep jockeying for space in our consciousness. The reality is that it often is very hard to control our thoughts.

Compared to controlling feelings and thoughts, controlling your language is much more practical and effective. You can decide to start speaking or to stop speaking. You can even decide with much greater control what type of words you choose to use among various types of phrasing or context. So it seems reasonable, as you will read many times in this book—of the three, *the easiest to control is your language.* And it is true that what you say does affect what you feel, which affects what you think.

TIRED OF TRIANGLES? . . . TRY THIS

We can diagram the interaction between your words, feelings, and thoughts in another way. On the left side we show what we would call the instigators, or in research terms, the independent variables. These are the items that combine to produce something. We may have a ways to go to completely understand the dynamic, but we can summarize these three as the cause portion in cause-effect analysis. Over to the right we see the effect portion of the analysis, which is the result, or behavioral, outcome. The tragedy in many lives is that when people see the result on the right-hand side, they have no idea what combination of events, thoughts, or actions came together to make it happen. They become superstitious, they blame others, they feel helpless as though they have no control over their own destiny or even their own day.

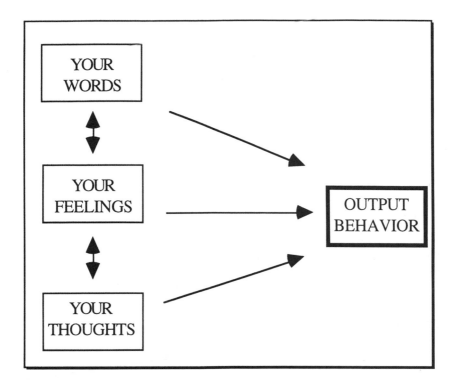

THE POWER OF WORDS

The power of words was illustrated to me many years ago when I was a senior in college. I had an old English BSA motorcycle. I was broke and this motorcycle was my only mode of transportation. It started making some strange noises, so I took it to a repairman by the name of Terry, who has since turned into a lifelong friend. Terry, a gentle, caring, and competent mechanic, looked at my motorcycle. I felt there was something seriously wrong, and I was worried that it would cost me a lot of money. The words in my mind were: "This is a disaster, this is awful, this is terrible, this is a catastrophe. I'm broke, and I won't have enough money to fix the motorcycle. My transportation will be finished."

Terry looked at the motorcycle and listened to its subtle thumping and warbling sounds. Looking back at me, he said, "This is simply going to be an irritation. This is natural when this particular type of motorcycle ages— this noise is normal."

I said, "What do you mean?"

He said, "This sound will simply be a nuisance."

The moment he said the word *nuisance*, my body relaxed. I could cope with the nuisance. I could deal with an inconvenience, but it would be very difficult for me to cope with a *disaster*.

At that point I became keenly aware of the sheer impact of words. If I started thinking of something as a nuisance, it was palatable; if it was a disaster, I couldn't live with it. As the behavior triangle shows, the words I was now using affected my anxiety.

BEHAVIOR—THOUGHTS SUMMARY

In 1991 I bought a new Nissan 300 ZX, a sporty, fast, and sleek automobile. It was black with black leather interior and chrome wheels. This was the first 300 ZX I'd ever bought. Prior to this time, I was reasonably convinced that there were very few of them on the road. Yet once I bought the car I noticed more and more of them on the road.

The question is: Did I start noticing more of them because I had started a trend and people were following my lead, or was it simply because I was looking for them? Would you say you noticed your brand of car more often after you'd bought the car? Chances are very good the answer is "yes"—because what you focus on expands. I am firmly convinced that you see what you believe. If you believe in UFO's, miracles, or angels, chances are very good that you'll start noticing events and impressions that confirm your belief. Perhaps this explains why the negative and hurtful episodes in the world seem to multiply. Fortunately, this same phenomenon applies to the productive side of things. As you embrace the obvious and multiply your options, a positive attitude will form. Now, continue to speak positive terms and surround yourself with words, feelings, and thoughts that do you some good. Then watch that good begin to expand. Like my zippy 300 ZX, you'll notice it often.

SUMMARY

To sum up the behavior triangle, it's important that you understand the value of managing the ingredients. The idea is to create an output in behavior that exponentially enhances your performance, that increases the value of your life, that adds more meaning and contribution to the world. The smart option is to influence the Behavior Triangle in the easiest possible way, and in a way that actually helps you change to an optimistic explanatory style. I conclude that the easiest way to affect the Behavior Triangle is simply to control the way you speak.

SMOOTHING OUT THE BUMPS
POINTS TO REMEMBER/THINGS TO DO

1. Whether making cookies or building careers, the mix of ingredients will influence the outcome.

2. Quite often, one single ingredient has more influence over the others.

3. The Language Inclusion Process stresses that the language ingredient is the power-packed influencer.

4. The Behavioral Triangle diagrams the elements that can lead to your optimistic attitude.

5. The mix in your triangle leads to your results and outputs.

6. Words have amazing power to quickly influence your feelings of coping or of impending disaster.

7. Choose words that show confidence and positive expectations—good stuff will usually follow.

8. Start noticing how you and others speak.

5

It's refreshing to discover something you can instantly use. Here's a device you can apply the moment you learn it. Have fun in putting it to use today.

THE START/STOP PRINCIPLE

—

The words to a popular song include "I'll be there for you" and continue "someone to face the day with." These lyrics, along with a pop melody and nice back-up harmonies, have made for a rather successful ditty. Although the tune may be catchy, is it possible that the words can subtly take us down a path toward fear and pessimism? Recall the Language Inclusion Process— what you *say* affects how you *feel*, which in turn has powerful influence over your *thinking*.

Here's a helpful way of seeing the simplicity of the process and anticipating how easy and useful it will be when you learn it and apply it to your life. I'll take the liberty to encourage you to remember that even the easy and simple things you learn take skill and discipline in order to properly use them at home or at work.

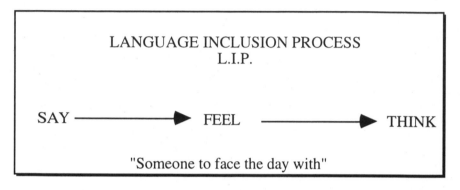

L.I.P. shows how the simple lyrics "someone to face the day with" can influence how a person feels later in the hour, day, or week. It's a catchy and even touching song, yet the selection of words can easily lead to a slight case of defensiveness and in an extreme example to feelings of impending doom. This is worth studying some more.

TRY SINGING THESE WORDS

The phrase "I'll be there for you . . . someone to *face* the day with" conjures up these issues that one might *face*:

    1. bills to pay
    2. chores to complete
    3. automobiles to repair
    4. taxes to compute/pay
    5. sense of fatigue

A very simple change in word selection can quickly direct your feelings and thoughts in a totally opposite direction—"I'll be there for you . . . someone to *enjoy* the day with" can prompt:

1. movie to watch
2. dessert to enjoy
3. coffee to savor
4. meals to devour
5. romance to cherish

It would be easy to say this is getting too detailed or that it's unnecessary to have to watch *all* that we say. That is correct for most people. However, those who are traveling down a path toward optimism, and who want to keep an attitude about life that sparkles, are open to the elements (or ingredients if you're making my famous cookies) that make it happen. Major outcomes are often determined by seemingly small details. The words in song lyrics repeated over and over will influence what happens in the listener's life sooner or later. Here's the cause-and-effect issue we discussed earlier. I hope your progression this far and throughout this book will open your eyes as to what makes you the type of person you are, and how you can control this result or outcome.

THE LANGUAGE OF *EXCLUSION*

Adults talk about what *is not* there and children talk about what *is* there. That means that adults have a language of exclusion. They almost always talk in deficit by describing what is missing, what is excluded, what is not there. They often describe their experiences, good or bad, in terms of what those experiences are *not*.

To illustrate this point, let's look at your reaction to this new bit of knowledge. You might have said: "I never think of those things" or "I would have never thought of that." It seems to be an adult thing (or at least after about age thirteen) to begin phrasing ideas with never, no, and not bad. An alternative would be: "This is the first time I ever thought about that." Or: "That's an exciting bit of new information." Notice now the feelings are those of interest and curiosity. You might also notice surprise and, perhaps, fascination.

ARE CHILDREN REALLY OPTIMISTIC?

Would you say that children ages four to twelve are more optimistic than pessimistic? When I've asked that question of thousands of people in my training and consulting sessions around the country, they have generally said that children are more optimistic.

Would you say that generally you notice that children are in a better mood than you? Have you noticed that when kids are in a good mood, their good mood reminds you that you are not in a good mood? Some adults will go so far as to respond to them by saying, "What's so funny?"

Sometimes we look at children who are in a good mood, who are optimistic, and we say, "Well, they haven't learned yet—they haven't concluded yet that life is a tough haul and it gets tougher. They're naive. They don't really understand that life is painful." We often discount or invalidate children's optimism possibly because they have yet to experience the life lessons that make some people negative. Children tend to pay attention to lots of experiences that help them remain optimistic. They look at cartoons on television, which are fun. They read comic books, which are fun. They read children's stories, and many children's stories are fun. It's almost as if young children give themselves a type of mental nourishment that tends to be positive.

DO WE HAVE TO COMPARE?

Now look at adults. Many adults read the newspaper every day, and most of the information it contains is bad news—people getting killed, people being lied to, people getting sick, disasters, financial crises, one catastrophe after another—a steady diet of bad news. The same is true when you turn on the radio and the television. But even when there is good news, it is positioned in exclusionary terms—terms of what isn't there. So good news as well as bad news can feed a negative, or pessimistic, style.

THE ALARM RINGS . . .

Imagine this example: You wake up in the morning when the alarm clock goes off, and bang, you start the day. You trudge out of bed and stumble to the bathroom. Along the way you turn on the television so you can catch the weather and traffic reports. You are blurry-eyed, looking in the mirror, slowly pulling yourself together, and you begin to listen to the morning's dose of bad news. Two people were killed in a car-jacking last night. Six were killed in a massive car accident hundreds of miles away. Last night a building burned downtown and arson is suspected. The state budget crisis is requiring teachers to be laid off. There are massive layoffs at the factory in the county. The Dow Jones Industrial average is going down. What a way to start the day!

Next the very cheery, very friendly, somewhat folksy weather person comes on. You notice that he is describing weather in terms of what it is not. He says, "Well, today won't be too hot, and when we look at the air quality, there won't be too much of a problem. If we look at the pollen count, there is not gonna be too much pollen in the air. All in all, it won't be a bad day." He describes this beautiful day in terms of there NOT being a problem, NOT being too hard on your eyes, NOT being too hard on your breathing, NOT being too threatening in terms of your allergies.

AND HOW IS THE WEATHER?

The weather person could say instead, "It's gonna be a beautiful day. The air will be clear. You'll breathe easy. The sun will be out for you to enjoy." However, he positions the nature of the beautiful day in terms of what it is not.

Let's back up for a moment. Remember the lyrics to our song at the beginning of this chapter? We replaced *face* the day with *enjoy* the day. You may notice a more direct connection with the weather example. This is because after your morning routine you will be dealing directly with the weather. Just like the words in the song, the words in the weather report will be digested by your mind. This is why some of us face each day defensively or get depressed about pollen, heat, and air quality on a totally beautiful day.

Now, the weather person hands his baton to the very friendly and very informative traffic reporter. She describes the morning commute as you anticipate climbing into your vehicle and fighting traffic. This morning she says, "Well, on Interstate 80 the traffic won't be too much of a problem today. As we look at the toll bridge, we see there is not too much of a backup at the metering lights. On Interstate 280 there is not too long of a backup coming into downtown as well."

The traffic reporter could say, "The traffic is smooth. You'll enjoy your commute into downtown. The cars are moving nicely through the metering lights." But she talks about good news in terms of what it is not. Not too big of a problem, not too much of a backup, not too large of an irritant.

As you've taken inventory of your day, you've gotten a huge dose of bad news and the good news has been positioned in terms of what's missing. If you get a steady diet of this every day for years, it is very difficult to have a strong self-concept and feel good about life. Later, our final chapter will explore an idealistic twist on this type of story.

I SHOULD DO WHAT?

Could it be that our language actually keeps us pessimistic? That's what I discovered several years ago. It is very difficult to just become optimistic. It is very challenging to just decide that you are going to be positive. There have been many times that you may have said to yourself, "I should be more positive. I should be happier. I shouldn't be so critical. I shouldn't feel so bad. I shouldn't feel so cynical. I shouldn't be so negative. I should just be positive." Unfortunately, even though you say things like this to yourself, it takes discipline and effort to make really positive changes. Please bear with me as I stress this point once again. It's like saving dollars or cutting calories off of the diet—both are relatively painless in moderate amounts but both become extremely difficult for large segments of the population. Common sense things are often hard to do.

HOW TO MAKE CHANGE STICK

It's quite tricky to just change your mind and have that mind-change stick. It's important to have some other device that is going to regularly influence the Behavior Triangle (Say-Feel-Think). A useful method is to change the way you speak.

It can be laborious to genuinely become optimistic, so you must have a reliable device that regularly influences your Behavior Triangle. That device is the Language Inclusion Process. You can learn how to change your language on a regular basis from what is missing to what is there. This change requires lots of practice and an acute awareness of how you speak in the first place. The good news is that your language is under your direct control. It may seem silly, and it will be hard at times, but as you experiment with the right amount, you'll find what works for you.

LET'S ASK MICKEY & THE GANG

If you go to Disneyland for the weekend, it's unusual to have a bad time. It is, after all, the "Happiest place on earth," and it is the "Magic Kingdom." The weather is wonderful as you spend the weekend with your children in Disneyland. You go on the rides, you look at all the attractions, you are awestruck by the ways in which the technology in the "Magic Kingdom" affects your mood. Notice that it is very unlikely in Disneyland, with all of the thousands of people who are there, that you ever see anybody fighting. There are people from all parts of the world, and they come in all shapes and sizes and colors. There are fat people and thin people, tall people and short people, black and white and yellow and red people, people from every nationality and many languages and wearing many costumes, and everyone seems to be having a very good time. It is truly a tall order to have a bad time in Disneyland.

So let's suppose you go to Disneyland and you have a wonderful time. I come up to you and ask, "How did you like Disneyland?" If your response is, "Not bad," that description of what is NOT will usually come across in a cool monotone barren of excitement or enthusiasm.

But what if you say, "Great!"? You'll notice that there is a difference in volume, in affect, in intonation—in the whole feeling associated with the word "great." Your volume goes up. Your mouth gets more relaxed. Your thoughts and feelings are quite different when you talk about what's there as opposed to what's missing.

That is the whole principle around the Language Inclusion Process—to get in the habit of talking about *what is there* (inclusion) as opposed to *what is missing* (exclusion). This can exert powerful influence on the Behavior Triangle and, quite frankly, change your life.

THE START/STOP PRINCIPLE

Okay, now that we're back from Disneyland, let's get into some basics. If you are interested in changing your behavior, it's important to develop a lever that will make you actually do it and a method that will make it easy to do. What is really curious about most adults is that they spend so much time, effort, and energy concentrating on methods that actually make change more difficult rather than easier.

One way to start learning to shift your language to an inclusion process is to understand and use the Start/Stop Principle.   In brief, this idea suggests that when it's difficult to *stop* certain behavior patterns, we should see if we can *start* new patterns.   This process gives us two advantages. First, the success rate of starting is much higher than stopping, and second, the offending behavior is eliminated as desired.

The Start/Stop Principle works like this: Most people are dissatisfied with certain behavior patterns they have. When they want to change, they concentrate on trying to *stop* an existing behavior, which, of course, makes them concentrate on that very thing.

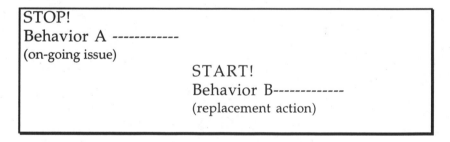

```
STOP!
Behavior A ------------
(on-going issue)
                    START!
                    Behavior B-------------
                    (replacement action)
```

Stop worrying, stop smoking, stop over-eating, stop being negative are examples.   Let's examine several of them so you can see what I mean.

Suppose you are a worrier. You tend to be anxious, you catastrophize a lot, you spend a fair amount of time being concerned about future possibilities. You wake up in the middle of the night agonizing about things. You give yourself an upset stomach. You can lose your appetite or eat a lot when you're worrying.

STILL WORRIED?

If you are a worrier, you are probably pretty good at it. You are very skilled at it because you practice it a lot, and it certainly takes up a lot of your time. Now, intellectually, I imagine you probably dislike worrying. You have probably said to yourself, "I should stop worrying," or your family members, your spouse, your friends, your siblings may have said, with the best of intentions, "You know, you should really stop worrying. There really is nothing to be so concerned about. You really shouldn't be so upset." The last thing on your mind is writing a thank-you note to the person giving you that advice.

One reason it is so difficult to change from worrying to something else is because you are concentrating on trying to STOP it. To STOP something means you're focusing on that thing—and remember, what you focus on expands. When you try to stop worrying, you feel worried, and then you start thinking about all the things that set you to worrying.

Look at the Behavior Triangle: What you say affects how you feel, which affects how you think. So now you have to ask yourself a question: Is it easier to stop worrying or is it easier to start learning how to relax? I'm sure you'll agree that intellectually it seems easier to start learning how to relax.

Let's take another example: Smoking. Most people will agree that smoking is bad for you. It's responsible for a lot of disease in our society, and it's considered by health professionals and insurance researchers as the number one preventable cause of death.

If you have smoked for a long time, you are, of course, very good at it. You may have tried to stop smoking on many occasions. If you finally did quit, you probably made several attempts before·you succeeded. Now, one of the reasons why it is so difficult to stop smoking is because you're addicted to it. However, ask yourself this question: What is easier, to stop smoking or to start regularly breathing clean air? It is easier, just in your mind, to concentrate on breathing clean air. Yet most people have trouble with quitting smoking because they are trying to stop. The moment they try to stop, they feel deprived.

At the risk of pushing too far, I'd like to go to the next subject: Weight. America is fat. Our society is more overweight than it has ever been. America has won the title of having the most obese population on the planet. According to recent studies, in the last decade America has gained at least eleven pounds per person. One in three Americans is now obese. Two in three are seriously overweight. Americans spend amazing amounts of money on weight reduction, buying diet books, diet aids exercise manuals. Well, most of America really doesn't have any trouble losing weight; what Americans have trouble with is keeping the weight off. Let's examine that.

Let's say you think you are overweight. You decide that Monday's a good day to start dieting, so you enjoy the last supper on Sunday. On Monday you STOP eating, denying yourself the very food that you want to eat. You STOP eating. After a period of time, days or weeks (or even hours), you feel deprived. The good news is you do lose some weight; the bad news is that you feel bad and you're cranky and you have lost energy. So to reward yourself, what do you do after you drop those few pounds? Well, you eat! Which, for many, means you gain all the weight back. This is known as the yo-yo effect.

Since diets so often fail, you have to ask yourself a question: What is easier, to stop eating or to start eating sensibly? The natural answer is it's easier to start eating sensibly. The reality is that it's easier to start a new behavior pattern than it is to stop an old behavior pattern. Yet most adults concentrate on behaviors that they want themselves or others to stop.

Where does L.I.P. fit into this discussion? Worrying, smoking, and dieting carry the baggage of broken promises, missed goals, and disappointing efforts. The Language Inclusion Process offers a way to control a piece of the puzzle that is controllable. What you say is the first tangible step you can take on the road to managing these behaviors. The Start/Stop Principle, connected with L.I.P., offers a unique twist on where to place your efforts so that you reach your goal.

The key message of Start/Stop is this: If you're interested in changing your behavior, if you're interested in learning a method that will change your explanatory style from pessimistic to optimistic, then, of course, you want to concentrate on starting a new behavior rather than stopping an old one. The beauty of the Language Inclusion Process is that when you concentrate on a new behavior that's easy to do, the counterproductive exclusionary habits will simply and naturally move aside. So instead of *stopping* your habit of speaking in terms of what's negative or missing, *start* speaking about the many positives that are often right in front of you.

SUMMARY

It's important to remember that starting a behavior pattern is easier than stopping an old one. It's easier to concentrate on starting to breathe clean air, starting to eat sensibly, starting to learn to relax, starting to concentrate on hitting the ball down the fairway, and starting to be more positive. To do that, you need to start practicing the Language Inclusion Process, and it will make wholesale changes in the way in which you think.

In the subsequent chapters I will be talking about all the dimensions in which the Language Inclusion Process can be applied—recovering from anger, achieving optimum performance, having more productive relationships. You will learn many ways to apply the Language Inclusion Process in different dimensions of your speech.

SMOOTHING OUT THE BUMPS
POINTS TO REMEMBER/THINGS TO DO

1. Begin to notice the positive and negative power of words.

2. Remember your words influence your feelings and your feelings will impact your thinking.

3. Children seem to have a natural attraction to an optimistic way of talking, feeling, and thinking.

4. An explanatory style based on exclusion focuses on what *is not* there.

5. An explanatory style based on inclusion focuses on what *is* there.

6. An inclusionary explanatory style helps your words, feelings, and thoughts to stay positive.

7. It is easier to start than to stop something.

8. Starting the Language Inclusion Process will replace the Language of Exclusion.

6

You control where you aim your focus. You may choose the up side or the down side—whichever you select, it will begin to enlarge and grow. You can center on your irrational fears or on the positive areas of growth.

HOW TO COMBAT
IRRATIONAL BELIEFS

—

I always marvel at how we are willing to work so hard on the wrong problem. Maybe it's the adrenaline or the feeling of accomplishment that makes us start a project and work quite diligently at it before we get the information we need to prepare to do it right.

There are many beautiful homes at Lake Tahoe, which separates Nevada and California where you see the 45-degree bend on the map. Many out-of-town architects design homes without taking into account the unforgiving local snowfall patterns. One beautiful home had a sharp-looking redwood deck with a railing off the main house. The problem was that the snow from the roof unloaded directly onto the deck. After piling up, it would break through the wood railing. It got so that merely driving by, I could predict when the snow would bust the railing down and pour off of the deck. The next spring I'd see stacks of new lumber for the repair job.

This repair job seemed quite irrational to me. It pointed to the need to fix the real problem once rather than fixing the result of the problem over and over. Often good ideas and relationships are discarded after some sticky issue has been supposedly "fixed." But if this issue is simply the result of a deeper problem (like a poorly designed house), the issue remains—it may be rebuilt, re-engineered, or replaced, but until the core problem is eliminated it will again produce the same result. It's insane for you, me, or that homeowner at Lake Tahoe to think that rebuilding the railing over and over will fix the problem.

SEE IT WHEN YOU BELIEVE IT

We have all heard the phrase, "I'll believe it when I see it." Let's switch the verbs around and see what happens. Can it be possible that you really do *see it* when you *believe it*?

When you become convinced of a certain belief system, your possessions around you reflect that belief. You will begin to organize your *reality* to reflect your way of thinking. The principle is that whatever you focus on expands! If you are particularly convinced of the superiority of your car over others, you will frequently see that brand of car on the road. If you are suspicious of the opposite sex, you will frequently find members of the opposite sex out there behaving in a way that confirms your suspicions.

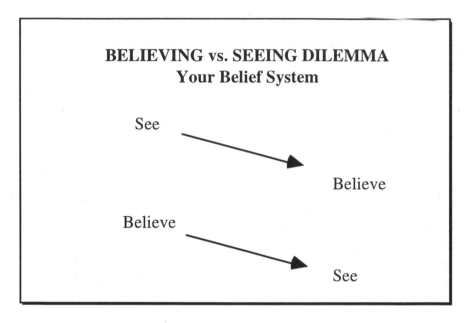

The conclusion here is that your belief systems define and determine your reality. It is entirely possible you have existing long-held beliefs in your mind that are counterproductive and self-defeating. As in our winter wonderland (Lake Tahoe story) earlier, it helps to spend time and effort on the correct portion of the problem so that we get the payoff for all that work. It becomes insane to work over and over on the wrong parts of a job only to redo it time and again. The reality is that many people reading this book fall into this trap. Let's see if we can better identify what is happening and come up with some rational ways of making lasting improvement.

Imagine there is a tape recorder in your head that is playing a series of tapes over and over again like the times when a song you've heard plays itself in your mind over and over until it drives you crazy. These mental tapes reinforce beliefs that are often irrational and counterproductive, yet they can be very pervasive.

An important thing to know here is how much time is wasted with the need to believe the irrational beliefs and then back them up with exclusionary speech. In order to adopt a new, more rational idea quickly, you must practice the inclusionary language, which is much more realistic and, therefore, more optimistic.

Albert Ellis, Ph.D., a founder of the cognitive method of psychology, is one of the most respected professionals in that field. The author of many articles and books, he created the Rational Emotive Method of Psychotherapy. This method suggests that your behavior is a result of your belief system. If your beliefs are counterproductive or irrational, then your behavior will follow suit. Regardless of how you try to alter your behavior on the outside, your beliefs on the inside dictate what you do. They are the origin of all the long-term routines in your ordinary behavior. According to Dr. Ellis, to achieve constructive change you must identify the irrational beliefs, question the irrational beliefs, dispute the irrational beliefs, and replace them with rational and productive beliefs. This may sound like a great deal of work, but it's worth it.

There are many irrational beliefs you might hold, but certain ones are particularly popular. Dr. Ellis calls them "The Eleven Irrational Ideas."

In this chapter I will outline the eleven irrational ideas and show how each is detrimental and self-defeating in your personal and work lives. We will look at how exclusionary language (what's not there) confirms and retains the irrational belief, and how inclusionary word choices (what's there) lead us toward a useful replacement of the belief.

The Eleven Irrational Ideas are:

1. Adults must always be loved.
2. Perfection is required for self-worth.
3. Certain types of people are all bad.
4. Everything is a catastrophe.
5. We have no control over happiness.
6. We must dwell on improbable dangers.
7. It's easier to avoid rather than face.
8. One should depend on someone stronger.
9. Our past keeps influencing present behavior.
10. One should be upset over other people's problems.
11. There is one right solution to human problems.

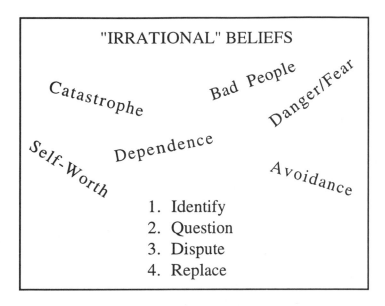

IRRATIONAL BELIEF 1: LOVE & APPROVAL

It is a dire necessity for an adult human being to be loved or approved of by every significant other person in the community.

It is impossible for everyone to love you or approve of you all the time. Emotionally, though, many people spend a good portion of their lives trying to achieve that status. It is normal to want the approval and affection of others. It gets out of hand when we spend considerable time ruminating on it or becoming inactive and dysfunctional because we fear that others don't love or approve of us.

As you examine this belief, you will notice that many people select exclusionary language to describe this belief.

- "Nobody loves me."
- "I'm nothing without you."
- "I'm not popular like everyone else."
- "I'll never fit in."

They become hostage to the approval of others so that they often have trouble functioning without that approval. Exclusionary language ensures that this problem will continue.

Often, as a result of these negative statements and the negative feelings that follow, people do some pretty counterproductive things—some will cheat, break the rules, over-accommodate, victimize themselves or others, and engage in other self-destructive behaviors.

An example is teenage girls who have sex with boys in the interest of being popular and liked by the boys. Young boys, searching for approval and peer acceptance, participate in drugs, in gang-related behavior, and in other self-defeating routines.

Some people have trouble saying "no" when people ask something of them. They harbor the illusion that the approval they so desperately need is more important than reasonable limits.

The first thing to do is to recognize the belief as "irrational and impossible." It is quite simply impossible to get everyone to like you or approve of you all the time. You can start by disputing the irrational belief and then replace it with a more reasonable and productive one.

Here is an example of a more reasonable and productive belief that you could adopt: "Some people will like me, some will love me, some will approve of me, and some will criticize me. Some will be confused by me. Some will disapprove. A whole bunch of people have yet to meet me and make up their minds. All of this is okay. I will be fine."

If you examine this new belief, it will appear to be more reasonable and appropriate. Now the question is: How on earth can you adopt this belief so it sticks in your mind and plays over and over again? Well, one of the most important things here is to change your language to one of inclusion. If you want this new belief to take hold, if you want to adopt it quickly, you need to change the words on the tape you are playing to yourself.

Listen to the difference that the language of inclusion makes: Instead of, "Nobody loves me," you can say, "Some people will love me." Instead of "I'm nothing without you," you can say, "I'm something when you're gone." Or, "I'm still somebody, regardless of how others feel about me." Here are a few other ideas:

- "I'm different than many other people."
- "I'm attractive and have my own look and style."
- "I fit in with people like me."
- "I'm as good as I am now, and I'm still learning and improving."

IRRATIONAL BELIEF 2:
PERFECTION & SELF-WORTH

One should be confident, adequate, and achieving in every possible respect if one is to consider oneself worthwhile.

This belief is very popular with anyone who is driven or highly motivated—an achiever, an obsessive, an entrepreneur. I have personally had trouble with this belief for a good portion of my life. Having spent many years working with high achievers, I've noticed that this belief is very popular (and self-defeating).

To explain: This belief says that you must at all times be clean, neat, trustworthy, loyal, brave, on top of it, bulletproof, knowledgeable, in control, strong, and free of mistakes; in short, perfect! And if for one moment there is a flaw, a mistake, a kink in the armor, an imperfection, then you are less worthwhile.

People who hold this belief spend enormous amounts of time compensating for their weaknesses by striving to pretend that they are invincible. Often we attempt to appear perfect and superhuman. Our exclusionary language regularly illuminates and amplifies this crazy belief:

- "I'm not good enough."
- "I never do anything right."
- "I don't deserve (whatever) because I haven't earned it."
- "It really wasn't my fault."

In seeking approval and reinforcement from others, we delude ourselves into thinking that it is our perfections that draw people to us. We think something like this: "If I appear perfect, then you will be impressed and drawn to me. In reality, though, what will happen is my perfections will remind you of your imperfections and, therefore, will scare and alienate you. My perfections are an estranging device because there is very little with which you can identify when you are reminded of perfection. In reality, if I show you my imperfections, my vulnerability, and my humanness, you are much more likely to feel more comfortable around me and, therefore, attracted."

Notice that exclusionary language nicely illustrates our tendency to abdicate responsibility (at times by taking on too much), reject accountability, and continue the need to appear bulletproof.

You must recognize, dispute, and replace your irrational belief with a rational and productive one. It's actually a relief to acknowledge mistakes and vulnerabilities since that acknowledgment is truthful and allows the pressure of perfection to be relieved. Here is an alternative to Irrational Belief Number Two: The Perfection Obsession.

"I will be confident and achieving in some areas and I will be marginal in others and completely ignorant in others. I have high standards and those standards are okay, and I'm still quite okay regardless of how many perfections and imperfections I have. Therefore, my worth is intact and I will continue to grow."

This new belief requires practice to be engraved in your mind. Then, of course, it's critical to change your language to one of inclusion. Notice how the previously negative remarks will sound with a slight change in language:

- "I will need to work on it some more to get it right."
- "I've made an error and I'm mistaken."
- "I have contributed to this problem."
- "I've done some stupid things and I've made some mistakes."
- "I'm embarrassed and defensive."

IRRATIONAL BELIEF 3: BAD PEOPLE

Certain people are bad, wicked, or villainous, and they should be severely blamed and punished for their villainy.

Everyone spends some time with this one. We have, after all, at one time or another been very upset and blamed an entire group of people for something. Sometimes when we are feeling immobilized or victimized or overwhelmed with the complexity of the world, we want to blame groups of people for our trouble. Most of the time, though, it is because we are upset and we want to vent our frustrations. When we continue with this thinking, we develop biases and prejudices that influence our behavior and actually create more conflict. Prejudices and biases abound everywhere: All Blacks are violent, all Arabs are evil, all Hispanics are lazy, all politicians are liars, all Caucasians are racists, all stockbrokers are greedy, all people on welfare are cheats, all graffiti artists are subhuman, all feminists are femi-nazis, anyone nonwhite should be exterminated, all Jews are tight, et cetera.

Perpetuating prejudice and bias keeps the problem alive and growing. Consider how your prejudices blossom the more you focus on how others are not like you. Prejudices and hate, if allowed to grow, actually make life more toxic for you. Notice what kind of a person you turn into when you spend so much time being judgmental and hateful of people who look and behave differently than you.

Consider the following replacement belief: "People come in different colors, races, creeds, dispositions and cultures. Some in every category are bad and defective, and some are wonderful, and many are in between. I will contribute best to the world by setting an example and having high standards, and I will accept and be willing to learn from people who are different than I." Concentrate on speaking in inclusion. Instead of speaking about how people are not like you, speak of how they are like you and how that can be a source of learning. It will help you notice what is there as opposed to what is missing. Capitalize on what is in existence and learn to get along with people different than yourself.

IRRATIONAL BELIEF 4: CATASTROPHES

It is awful and catastrophic when things are not the way one would very much like them to be.

This belief is an especially popular one for people who are into trauma and catastrophes. Many who habitually have tantrums and feelings of agony will use this idea to justify being histrionic and demonic. It's so curious that many of us actually seem to prefer being upset. When things turn out differently than we planned, we frequently get so anxious that it seems like a condition we're opting for. Of course, our regular exclusionary language actually strengthens this irrational belief and makes it worse:

- "My outfit did not come back from the cleaners, and I have nothing to wear."
- "There are no reservations available. What will we do?"
- "You are late. We will never get to the plane on time."
- "The food's cold, and it won't taste right."
- "This traffic jam will never let up."
- "No one wants to buy it. What will I do?"

These statements sound very familiar. So often when something does not turn out right, we start agonizing. The exclusionary language really helps the severity to become extreme, and we can sometimes feel quite justified in feeling victimized. It becomes a perfect opportunity for self-pity and feeling sorry for yourself.

Ask yourself how much you want to continue to believe this idea; further, you have to start deciding what you are going to believe instead. Consider the following replacement belief—the idea that if something turns out differently than you planned, it may be a nuisance or an inconvenience, yet it is still manageable with some learning and patience. Check your language here. Make sure you're using inclusion on a regular basis to help you anchor the new idea and reduce the worrisome tendencies of the old idea. Consider the following replacements:

- "My outfit is still at the cleaners. I'll have to find something else to wear.
- "Reservations are filled. Where else shall we go?"
- "You are late and it will be difficult to make the plane."
- "The food has cooled off. Let's see how it tastes."
- "This traffic jam seems to be a long one."
- "The products have yet to sell. I will look at my options."

Notice that inclusionary language really takes the severity out of the statements and, therefore, calms down the drama, the agony, the histrionics, and the anxiety. Recovery is much more assured. The objective here is if you want to accept a new, more rational belief into your life, something has to make it stick. When your speech patterns regularly include inclusionary language, you improve the chances of staying with the new belief.

IRRATIONAL BELIEF 5: HAPPINESS

Human unhappiness is externally caused, and people have little or no control over their sorrows and disturbances.

Once again, this idea is very popular. As they get older, children adopt this idea as a matter of course. Adults often use this one to avoid taking responsibility for their feelings, positions, and behavior. You may notice how often you will blame external circumstances for your own behavior, and you may find that your talk about what is missing is actually an accomplice in strengthening this belief.

- "I can't help it. You made me mad."
- "I had no choice. You left me with no alternative."
- "You never let me do anything I want to do."
- "I did not want to, but they made me upset."
- "I would not have done it, but she was not there to tell me not to."

This is unfortunate thinking. Our society is skilled at whining about how everyone else is always to blame. I would think that sooner or later we would grow up and take some personal responsibility. Yet as long as there appears to be the ability to create frivolous lawsuits and the victim mentality, I suppose we will continue to blame everyone else.

The real message remains that if I can blame some other people, I will. I am not in command of my behavior as long as I have someone else to give the responsibility to. What is really appalling is how the legal system now clearly reinforces this notion of someone else always being responsible. Certainly, if there is money in it, people will continue to avoid responsibility and continue to take advantage.

So take responsibility for yourself and reword your beliefs. Consider the following: "My happiness and my unhappiness are caused by me. I have lots of control over my experiences, disturbances, and misfortune." Then use inclusionary language on a regular basis to anchor this new belief in your mind and to result in corresponding behavior.

- "I'm angry with you, but I will control myself."
- "I have many choices, and I have several alternatives."
- "Rarely do you let me do anything I want to do."
- "These people are very upsetting, but I'll choose to do something else."
- "Though she was elsewhere, I chose to do it anyway."

These inclusionary remarks are more realistic and more likely to lessen the entitlement or victim mentality that is so popular in our society.

IRRATIONAL BELIEF 6: DANGER

If something is or may be dangerous or fearsome, one should be terribly concerned about it and dwell on the possibility of it occurring.

The person who has this belief is a worrier, a crisis-junkie, a type of agonizer. Many people find this belief very familiar and are worrying all the time about one thing or another. Sometimes when you really get into this idea, you become consumed to the point where your health becomes at risk. My education and practice as a therapist confirmed that anxiety disorders are the most common of the psychological problems. Medications are frequently prescribed for these problems, but often they simply calm down the symptoms while leaving the root belief system to remain working its irrational, maladaptive routine.

Moreover, consider the way our exclusionary language amplifies and inflames the world condition:

- "I'm not sure what will happen, and I just don't know what to do."
- "You just can't trust anyone these days, so don't talk to strangers."
- "There are not any jobs out there, and I got laid off, so I might as well sit here and not look for anything better."
- "It's not safe, so I never go out alone."
- "I read about an airplane crash, so I never fly."
- "I can't stop thinking about crime and being robbed."

There are any number of these types of remarks that come out of people who like to hang on to irrational beliefs. It is extremely difficult to get a worrier to stop worrying. Whenever you tell a worrier, "You really should not worry so much; there is nothing to worry about; there is no reason to be upset," you increase his or her feelings of insecurity and being out of control. Consider nudging him or her toward action and activities focused on what is present and real. Try suggesting that the worrier focus on a useful and current activity or a positive outcome of the situation.

IRRATIONAL BELIEF 7: AVOIDANCE

It is easier to avoid rather than face certain life difficulties and self-responsibilities.

This belief is probably the most popular of the whole list. I've noticed there are more people who believe this one than any other. And it certainly is easy to believe because at first glance it does seem to be easier to avoid problems than to face them. We often formulate elaborate methods for avoiding our challenges. We stall, pretend, procrastinate, and delude ourselves at just about every turn. Much time and energy are wasted with our stalling. Whether the problem is resolving conflicts with our family members, paying our taxes, getting in shape, or facing up to obligations, we always seem to find ways to put it off, and our exclusionary language certainly helps the delay.

- "Let's not talk about it right now it will probably work out in time."
- "I didn't know what to do first, so I didn't do anything."
- "I don't know where to start because I'm tired and I think right now a nap would be best."
- "They will never accept me, so why should I try?"
- "I know that I need to exercise and change my diet, but today is not a good day to start."

Actually, it is really *more* difficult to avoid problems than to confront and address them. You will spend more time and more energy with avoidance, rather than less.

When you deal directly with what you've been avoiding, you will find that the issue that you were agonizing about is a lot less frightening. Facing the music is in fact easier.

Rewrite the belief as follows: "It is easier to face rather than avoid certain life difficulties and self-responsibilities." To certify that this new belief will become anchored in your mind, you should change your language, once again, to inclusion.

- "Let's talk about it now, so it will be resolved sooner."
- "It was difficult to decide where to start, so I just started anywhere."
- "Though I'm having trouble deciding when to start, I think I'll start now."
- "I'm going to try regardless of how I'm received."
- "I know I need to exercise and change my diet, and now is as good a time as any to start."

Inclusionary language increases the likelihood of action and result. Whining goes down, accountability goes up, optimism begins to engage, and your personal control and growth are ensured.

IRRATIONAL BELIEF 8: DEPENDENCE

One should be dependent on others and need someone stronger than oneself on whom to rely.

This belief is very popular with people who want to get rescued or somehow "saved." Certainly many elements of our society have promoted this idea for years to the female gender. Depending on the role (dominant, submissive, wage earner, homemaker), many men and women play this belief out with surprising predictability.

The notion that you should be dependent is one of the best ways to ensure weakness for yourself and resentment toward the very person or institution on whom you are dependent. You end up disliking yourself and the other person or party you depend on. There are many marriages where one person has opted for financial and emotional dependence on the other. When this happens, and you are the one excessively depending on a spouse, you are reminded of your own weakness. This is often quite uncomfortable. As a result, you become very angry, critical, withdrawn or depressed. It appears easier to resent the person on whom you are dependent with the illusion that he or she has "robbed you of your strength."

If you have adopted this impotency crutch, you are constantly hostage to the whims and decisions of another, and, therefore, you have set yourself up to be very unhappy. Your exclusionary language ensures that you will be handcuffed to this dependency walking stick.

- "Now that you're not going, I can't go."
- "I can't go to the party by myself. Will you go with me?"
- "I'm not good at talking to those officials. Will you please talk to them for me?"
- "If you're not going to be here this weekend, I don't know what I will do."
- "I never had to work to support myself, and I think I should not have to change the life-style to which I have become accustomed."

If you want to continue the belief, then you deserve to be unhappy. However, assuming you've concluded that the dependency belief is counterproductive, then rewrite the belief. Consider this idea: Independence is central to mental health, and with it comes interdependence. Interdependence is the condition of independence with the ability to share. The moment you decide to believe, this is the moment you take charge of your life. Then the likelihood of giving becomes greater than the likelihood of taking.

Inclusionary language is essential here. Consider the following inclusionary statements to replace the old tape:

- "Now that you're going to stay, I'm going to go anyway."
- "I'm nervous about going to the party by myself, but I'm going to go anyway."
- "I'm going to talk to those officials in spite of my anxiety about doing it."
- "If you're going to be elsewhere this weekend, I'll learn to do something in your absence."
- "This is the first time I've had to support myself, and it's time I learned how to do it."

Though this language is a lot less romantic than most of the popular songs out these days, it still has a wholesale impact on that crutch or walking stick we referred to that always has you leaning on another person. Adjusting what you say, aloud and to yourself, will dramatically increase independence and move you toward a stronger self-concept.

IRRATIONAL BELIEF 9: PAST CIRCUMSTANCES

One's previous history is an all-important determiner of one's present behavior. Because something once influenced one's life, it should indefinitely have a similar effect.

This idea is very fashionable with a lot of people throughout the world. This belief is the foundation of the classic line: "That is just the way I am." We often resist trying to change our behavior, particularly if the behavior is counterproductive. If there is some convenient justification to continue our antisocial or harmful behavior, we will use it. In reality this statement suggests, "That's the way I've been and that is the way I've behaved in the past; I've gotten familiar with this routine; it has become a habit; I obtain some validation for my identity because of this; and I'm unaware of any new or easy methods for changing right now, so I'll just use the same convenient excuse."

If you want to change your behavior, you can. However, in addition to deciding that you want to, you will also have to develop skills to ensure that your behavior really is likely to change. Exclusionary language discourages any likelihood of changing, because in addition to the natural pessimism that emerges, such words can also kill any initiative.

- "I don't like it either. There is no way I can be different."
- "There isn't a prayer that I can change."
- "Listen, I'm not educated, so I can't."
- "I'm not used to those big words."
- "I'm Black, and you just don't know what it's like."
- "I'm Jewish. You have no idea what I've been through."
- "I'm Hispanic, so they will never give me a break."

- "I'm female, so I'm not given the same chances."
- "I'm a white male and everything's stacked against me. So there's no point in trying."

You certainly may have experienced negative or positive events based on your being a member of one of the above groups. The important thing for you to remember is that in addition to being responsible for how you interpret those past events, you are also responsible for your present behavior and reactions to all situations. Remember, too, that the way you speak has many side effects on your feeling and thinking. Try these:

- "I have trouble with it, and yet I'm going to be different."
- "It's going to be difficult for me to change, but I'm going to do it anyway."
- "Listen, although my education is limited, I'm still going to try it."
- "I have trouble using those sophisticated words."
- "I'm Black, and at times it gets rough."
- "Being Jewish has meant some good news and some difficult news."
- "As I'm Hispanic, it's sometimes harder to get a break."
- "I'm female, which sometimes adds pressures."
- "Okay, white males have new challenges, just like other groups."

IRRATIONAL BELIEF 10: OTHERS' PROBLEMS

One should become quite upset over other people's problems and disturbances.

This belief is one that is very popular with certain cultures or close-knit families. Although these groups have many good and admirable values, this belief carries a few unwanted side-effects. An attitude rooted in these groups says that the only way I can show you that I care is to be upset when you're upset. In other words, caring means being disturbed and is communicated through agonizing. Should you refrain from being upset, you're accused of caring too little.

This is both crazy and self-defeating. If you really think about it, you can certainly show lots of care, sympathy, empathy, compassion, and understanding without resorting to agonizing and being upset.

Can you imagine how I would have managed in my private practice of psychotherapy had I decided to get upset every time a patient was unhappy? At this point I would still be on medication for stress disorders—I might have developed heart disease and would probably have been hospitalized. Listen to these unreasonable exclusionary remarks that you may say if you hold this irrational belief:

- "You just don't care enough about what is going on."
- "I just can't relax if I know that you're not happy."
- "You know I can't go to sleep if I know that you are upset."
- "How can you possibly not do anything when you know he is not getting along with his wife."
- "You obviously don't care enough or you wouldn't be so insensitive."
- "I can't believe you don't even care that I lost my job."

Many family members control each other by using these statements. If you can think back into your past, you can probably recall situations where you either believed the idea or had it handed to you by someone, and as a result it may have affected much of your life. Consider this rewrite: You can be empathetic and understanding of another's problems and disturbances and still refrain from being upset yourself. Make sure to use the Language Inclusion Process to anchor this new belief.

- "I would appreciate seeing more actions that show you care."
- "I'm concerned that you are unhappy. What will you do about your situation?"
- "I'm going to relax. Can I do anything to help you calm down?"
- "How is it that you are able to be understanding and calm when you know he is having marriage troubles?"
- "Your caring about this seems less because you're calm and I'm upset."
- "I lost my job, so I guess I'll look for a new one tomorrow."

You'll see that the guilt manipulation is significantly reduced when you change your word selection.

IRRATIONAL BELIEF 11: POLARIZATION

There is a right, precise, and perfect solution to human problems, and it is catastrophic if that perfect solution is not found.

This last idea is what I call the "Felix Unger syndrome." This is from the television situation comedy involving two roommates—one is a slob and the other, Felix, is excessively compulsive in his neatness and cleanliness. It's the idea that perfection and simple, perfect answers are the only way to live. Certainly you can imagine what happens when you decide to believe this idea. You are now ripe for tantrums, stress problems, histrionics, explosions, depressions, and anxiety attacks.

What is at the root of this belief is the conviction that in any situation, there are only two options: right/wrong; win/lose; all/nothing; success/failure; perfect/flawed. This is an illogical, yet a very popular, idea.

Most adults tend to define everything in terms of such polar opposites. This polarization is often an unconscious reflex and the exclusionary language we use reinforces it. Some of the following remarks are common:

- "There is not any reason why we can't solve this easily."
- "There is only one right answer, and I won't rest until I find it."
- "There is no excuse for failure."
- "There is nothing we can't do to fix this."
- "If we don't solve this, we won't be able to succeed."
- "If we don't find it, I just don't know how we will do it."

Again, what to do? Well, start by disputing the belief and then rewrite it. You will recall from Chapter Two that there are multiple options and solutions to any problem. The key is to create the options, find some solutions that might fit, and move ahead.

When you consider the value of multiple options, a whole new world opens up. The win/lose mentality goes out the window, and you now can recover from the problem with movement of some kind. Consider how the Language Inclusion Process will help you adopt this idea.

- "We can solve this by looking at our options."
- "There are multiple options and I want to examine them."
- "Failure is an option that I want to resist. I would like to look at something else."
- "There is 'everything' we can look at to fix this."
- "If we solve this, we will be able to succeed."
- "If we continue to have trouble finding it, we will have to think of something else to do."

SUMMARY

We started this chapter with snow on a deck and our seeing vs. believing dilemma. In the first case, we saw that we often jump too soon and work feverishly on the wrong solution. In the second, we realized that if our beliefs are faulty and misdirected, it's hopeless to think that the outcome will be positive or productive. I hope this survey of irrational beliefs opens your eyes so you can see the real issues. If you trust the replacement beliefs and their positive outcomes, your life will become a solid example of seeing it when you believe it.

Our language makes our misdirected behavior continue by anchoring the irrationality of our belief. After the rewritten healthy belief has been outlined, you can proceed to fix the true issue rather than continue to repair the damaged deck railing every winter.

SMOOTHING OUT THE BUMPS
POINTS TO REMEMBER/THINGS TO DO

1. Keep looking for the rational cause of the challenge.

2. Try believing first and then look forward to seeing.

3. Refrain from giving irrational beliefs any additional support or foundation for their continued existence.

4. Fight back and refute the beliefs you recognize as being false.

5. Replace your irrational beliefs with those that are positive and based on what is present and real.

6. Continue to double-check your belief patterns. We often become lax with new beliefs that need support (or of old ones that creep back in).

7. Select language options that focus on what is there rather than on what is missing.

8. Remember to look for multiple options.

The Word on Chapter

7

How do you wrap classical music, anger, and getting fired into one bundle? This section does just that! As we continue forward we will find powerful ways of harnessing anger and putting it to good, positive use.

RECOVERING FROM ANGER

—

A friend of mine tells the story of how he discovered the amazing power of the brain and how it works with whatever we put in it. He says he had set a goal to learn to recognize and appreciate more classical music. While doing other activities he would put on some Bach, Brahms, or Telemann and read the titles as the pieces played on his compact disk player. He did this while eating, relaxing, and even before falling asleep at night. One evening he played Mozart's Piano Concerto #21 in C Major. He was moved by the opening *allegro*, transported by the *andante,* and thrilled by the closing *allegro vivace.* He could feel the musical genius of Mozart, but had trouble remembering the simplest of the melodies in any of the pieces. Although he considered himself musically challenged, he had hoped to remember some of what he had heard. This confused and disappointed him. One morning he got a surprise. Suddenly and without effort he noticed the melodies, especially the *andante,* rumbling around in his head. He ran back to his room, put the CD into the player, and quickly fast-forwarded to the middle section. To his amazement, he had recalled the main melodies and several of the harmonies as well. From then on, he respected the power of what goes into the brain and the results and actions that are bound to emerge.

Many people today seem to be confused as their definition of family changes and as the work world delivers less of the stability earlier generations enjoyed. If you watch television, read the newspaper, or listen to the radio, so often we are being shown pictures (or having scenes described) of people who are agitated on every continent. Their homes have sometimes been destroyed, their lives have been compromised.

It sure seems that the world is getting smaller as the population of the world is getting larger. Certainly if people are put into positions where they have to compete for more space or more resources, they are likely to get anxious. Surprisingly often, we notice on various television shows politicians being angry at each other, pointing fingers at each other, blaming each other or blaming certain systems. The media very often do interviews and sound bites with people illuminating how much they want to blame someone else for their anger. People are filing lawsuits in record numbers.

As I travel regularly around the world on airplanes and live in hotels, I meet interesting people. I can tell quickly who's carrying a grudge simply by looking at body language and encountering their energy. The people who are uptight have strong lines in their faces, they appear tense, they often have an accusatory nature and tone about them and they are generally unpleasant to be around.

I've also observed that children get angry quickly, yet recover fast. Adults seem to take much longer to recover from being angry.

THIS IS PERSONAL

My mother, though a very bright and wonderful woman in many respects, was often bitter and critical. She had trouble clarifying the events in her life that she perceived as unjust, and as a result she was usually tense and uneasy. I cared deeply for my mother, and when she passed away, I reflected on the hunch that if she had been able to clear up some of those perceived injustices, her life would have been more fulfilled and pleasurable. She might even have lived longer.

Being angry takes a huge physical toll. It has a toxic influence on people's relationships and also affects their self-concept. Ask yourself the questions: "When you are critical, condemning, uptight, do you like who you are? Do you like the person you turn into when you're angry?" I know that I don't, and I can be as upset as the next person.

Anger is a perfectly natural emotion and can manifest itself in a myriad of ways. Some of the ways are healthy and productive, and some others can be quite unhealthy and damaging. One point to remember is that past experiences with anger will linger—quietly at times or loudly at other times—and they will affect how you view your life and your world.

MORE IDEAS ON ANGER

Here's something to ponder: In a situation where you became angry, would you say the reason that made you angry changed by the fact that you got angry? Did you become destructive to yourself? Destructive to others? Both? Were you pleased about how you got angry, or afterward did you feel guilty and stupid? Did you feel proud of your behavior, or did you have regrets and remorse? Did you become violent? Did you have outbursts? Did you explode and then feel horrible after your explosion? Or did you implode and find yourself stomaching your anger? When you did that, did you find yourself eating a lot or losing your appetite? Did you find yourself creating ulcers, having to take medication, popping antacids and the like? After you have been angry, did you conclude that you could have been different, knowing what you know now?

When you're angry, do you really think you can control your behavior? Do you tend to think that anger is off limits? When you actually get angry, are you aware of it at the time? Some people are unaware.

Now, on one hand, some of you have real trouble getting angry at all. Somehow you were brought up with the idea that anger is off limits and unthinkable for a civilized person. Uncultured and uncontrolled people get angry, but nice people, refined people, don't get angry at all. Friends have learned that your tolerance for abuse is high, and they build that tolerance into the requests they ask of you and the events and situations they put you in. They are still your friends, but they just happen to know that you're not one they need to worry about—you keep from being angry.

On the other hand, some of you are anger experts. You have trouble stopping angry feelings from arising and exploding. As a matter of fact, you seem to be angry most of the time. People can tell when you are an angry person. I sometimes meet people who look like they're ready to blow up at a moment's notice. It's not their gender or ethnicity that gives it away. Neither is it the car they drive or where they live. One sure clue is the words they use to describe situations. Some use harsh and hurtful words, while others select calming and respectful kinds of statements. In my work I encounter wonderful people of all shapes and colors and sizes, from black men and women to white women and men to Jews and Catholics to Hispanics to Middle Easterners, to just about everybody. Unfortunately, some look like they're ready to get angry at a moment's notice, and some others are openly friendly and wear broad and easy smiles on their faces.

Most people dislike themselves when they are angry, in large part because they associate bad experiences with angry feelings. Most of the time when you're angry, the following feelings tend to surface:

- Betrayal
- Sabotage
- Rejection
- Inadequacy
- Jealousy
- Insecurity
- Humiliation
- Embarrassment

- Criticism
- Revenge

Now, consider those feelings and the situations you were in when you had them. I imagine you really felt badly about yourself, the situation, the circumstances, the aftermath, and very possibly your behavior throughout. If you disliked your behavior, think about how often it affects your self-esteem.

You may be like most people and generally admit that you often want to cool down when you're angry before you do something stupid that you would later regret. Think about how often you acted out of anger and regretted it later: The times when you exploded on somebody and brutalized them; the times when you hit the wall or broke a window or broke some object; the times when you really unloaded and criticized someone and humiliated them in public; the times when you ridiculed a group of people or said some particularly hateful things that afterwards you wish you had withheld; the times when you wrote nasty letters and made the mistake of mailing them before you waited overnight to read them again; the times when you were physically violent or acted out of jealous rage, only to be embarrassed and humiliated when you reviewed your behavior in the aftermath.

DOES ANGER MOTIVATE YOU?

Yet there are times when you are motivated by anger and are pleased by your actions. There are times when you need to have enough drive to get off your backside, and anger gives you the necessary stimulus.

Recall the times you have been depressed and frightened and then you finally became tired of being depressed and you got mad. Only then did you write that confronting letter or make the phone call or take the necessary step to face up to that intimidating person and get command back. Unexpressed anger and depression are a combination I often recognize in therapy or in relationships with clients. It's true that anger can often be the influence that helps depressed people recover. It can provide the horsepower to get people moving and help them remove themselves from a "blue funk."

In summary, anger is a very natural emotion. It happens to all people and it happens throughout their lives. It can be destructive, it can be self-destructive, it can be productive, it can be healthy. But how can you tell the difference between productive anger and the destructive type? Further, is there a way to control anger so that it can be healthy and motivating most of the time? And most important, is there a way to recover quickly from anger, particularly when anger is destructive? If you don't like who you are when you're angry, is there a way to return to the person whom you like?

Consider how language influences our feelings, particularly our feelings of anger. Now, remember the Behavior Triangle: Your language affects your feelings, which affect your thoughts, and vice versa. Have you ascertained that you have more regular and direct control over your language than the other two, your feelings and thoughts? Is it possible that with control over your language, you can actually shape the nature of your anger and your angry feelings? I'm convinced this is true.

If you examine your normal exclusionary language, it's always about absence, what's missing, what's not there. Now, when you're talking about deficits, think about how you feel. You might feel ripped off, betrayed, deprived, irritated. The more you think about it, the more you realize that exclusionary language might actually set you up to feel angry. It's entirely possible.

RIPPED OFF, BETRAYED, DEPRIVED

Examine the words *ripped off, betrayed, deprived*, and notice that when you say those words, there is a feeling that something is missing. You've been ripped off of your dignity; you have been betrayed and therefore you have lost face or you've lost money; you've been deprived of something. Most of the time the anger is a feeling that something is being compromised. Your dignity is being lessened, your self-respect has been removed, your perception of control over your life has been diluted.

Think about how many people in the country seem to be angry much of the time: the feminists, African-Americans, Jews, the homeless, white males, union members, social activists, the ACLU, the Ku Klux Klan. Many feel there is something missing in their lives. Large numbers have the victim mentality that seems to be so popular in this country these days. I know this sounds a little harsh and the reality is that we can all place ourselves in some group that does a lot of complaining. Listen to how we all talk when we are angry, and you'll notice that we are almost always talking in exclusion. While there may be very many legitimate issues around which we are complaining, somehow it seems we are more willing to blame other people and institutions than we are willing to take responsibility for ourselves and our own behavior. It seems that this is the current fad—to be angry, to scream discrimination, to blame it on someone else, and often to file a lawsuit. But before we criticize others too heavily, we must all take a look in the mirror.

I wonder what would happen to all these people who are so angry and blaming and kicking and screaming if they were to change their language from exclusion to inclusion? Might they begin looking at existence rather than absence? Might they become less pessimistic and more optimistic? Might they become less destructively angry and more oriented to engaging solutions rather than describing problems? Might they take more responsibility for their dilemmas and begin taking productive action?

Let's look at the process of how pessimism and anger mix. Remember how you feel when you are angry, deprived, ripped off, betrayed, foolish, embarrassed, humiliated, etc. In short, something has been missing or removed, left out, compromised; something is not there. You talk about it in your language. Examples are common:

- "I can't believe they did that."
- "They can't do that to me."
- "Now I'm left here with nothing."
- "He does not know whom he's talking to."
- "I've been ripped off of all my dignity."
- "These people have no concern for others."
- "I did not measure up to the standard."
- "I was not told the truth and I have lost everything."
- "I'm mad as hell and I'm not going to take it anymore."
- "They do not have any women on the panel."
- "They do not have any minority representatives."

- "They have not been concerned the slightest with our problems."
- "They just don't understand what I've gone through."
- "You could not possibly understand the trouble I've seen."

Does this sound familiar? These are all common remarks reflecting common situations where we feel angry. *Notice how much these remarks are based in exclusion.* Consider that exclusionary language, because it perpetually focuses on what is missing, actually encourages you to stay angry. Remember, when we focus on what's missing, it is very likely that we will continue to feel deprived.

JET FUEL FOR ANGER

The real message here is that exclusion and anger go together to make more anger. Therapy designed to get out hostility in people often makes hostile people more hostile. Imagine a situation in which you have been very angry. If you keep focusing on it, you will get upset all over again. Now spend five minutes speaking about the situation. You'll notice that as you describe the event that made you upset, you will begin feeling tense, your language might well be exclusionary, and you will become more tense. The conclusion here is that exclusionary language helps people become pessimistic, which fuels more anger, which makes more exclusion, which makes more pessimism, which makes more anger, etc. *Exclusionary language is jet fuel for the plane of anger.*

RECOVERING FROM ANGER
THROUGH THE USE OF L.I.P.

When you're angry, do you know the difference between when the anger is productive and you like who you are, and when the anger is detrimental and you don't like who you are? Most people will agree that when they're angry they want to recover from it. We know that exclusionary language increases the likelihood that anger will be destructive. We also know that inclusionary language encourages the development of optimism, and optimism is certainly likely to help you recover from anger. We also know that anger and pessimism go very well together. Therefore, *it follows that the use of L.I.P. will probably help you recover from the state of counterproductive anger.*

Let's re-examine these. Try saying all of them aloud:

- "I can't believe they did that."
- "They can't do that to me."
- "Now I'm left with nothing."
- "He does not know whom he's talking to."
- "I've been ripped off of all my dignity, and now I'm left with nothing."
- "These people have no concern for others."
- "They do not measure up to the standard."
- "I'm mad as hell and I'm not going to take it anymore."
- "They do not have any women on the panel."
- "They do not have any minority representatives."
- "They have not been concerned the slightest with our problems."
- "You just don't understand what I've gone through or the trouble I've seen."

As you say them out loud, I imagine you can really feel the emotions associated with anger multiply. Feelings like deprivation, humiliation, embarrassment, ridicule, self-pity, discrimination, rage, etc. With these feelings come the thoughts that back them up, and these thoughts express themselves in language that reinforces the feelings. It's a vicious cycle.

Now change each of those phrases or comments to inclusionary remarks.

- Instead of saying, "I can't believe they did that," say, out loud, "I'm surprised that they did that."
- Instead of "They can't do that to me," say, "They may regret doing that to me."
- Instead of "And now I'm left with nothing," say, "And now I'm left with very little."
- Instead of "He does not know who he's talking to," say, "He is unaware of who he's talking to."
- Instead of "I've been ripped off of all my dignity," say, "My dignity has been compromised."
- Instead of "These people have no concern for others," say, "These people have quite an unfeeling attitude about others."
- Instead of "They do not measure up to the standard," say, "They measured up to less than the standard."
- Instead of "I'm mad as hell and I'm not going to take it anymore," say, "I'm mad as hell and I'm going to do something about it."
- Instead of "They do not have any women on the panel," say, "They need some women on the panel."

- Instead of "They do not have any minority representatives," say, "They need minority representatives."
- Instead of "They have not been concerned in the slightest with our problem," say, "They have yet to show any concern about our dilemma."
- Instead of "You could not possibly understand what I've gone through," say, "It's very difficult for you to understand just what I've gone through."
- Instead of "You could not possibly understand the trouble I've seen," say, "Understanding the trouble I've been through will take some doing."

Notice the huge contrast in your feelings between the exclusionary remarks and the corresponding inclusionary remarks. Notice how the mere change to inclusion on the same statement changes the feeling from one of inaction to one of action, to more accountability. The counterproductive feelings of self-pity, cynicism, and deprivation are diminished dramatically.

Recall an experience that made you angry. Tell a story about it, keeping the entire story in exclusion. Talk about what did not happen, what was missing, what was absent. Notice how you feel. And then you will recall more thoughts that will heighten the angry feelings.

For example: Suppose you were recently fired from your job. You felt it was unjust and not fair. Telling the story out loud, you say something like this: "Well, I don't have my job anymore. That's right. I was recently fired, and I don't know what I'm going to do. I'm not going to be able to pay my bills, and I don't know how I'm going to be able to handle the taxes. I don't know what I'm going to tell my children. I have no idea how I'm going to be able to handle the mortgage. We're not going to have a good Christmas. I'm not going to be able to take care of all my obligations. I just don't know what I'm going to do. I don't know what I'm going to do."

Now when you say all of this, notice how frustrated and powerless you feel. If you add to it, you can continue the remarks by saying, "These people had no right to fire me the way they did. They had no idea what I was doing, and what they thought wasn't at all the truth. They didn't tell me what I would really be accountable for, and they never talked with me along the way. All they did was fire me, and they had no concern about what this was going to mean to me. These people have no feelings at all, particularly since Christmas is coming up."

Observe that when you continue to speak in exclusion, the anger escalates and the thoughts just build on themselves.

Now tell the same story again, but this time use the language of inclusion. You will notice that your words and feelings are slightly different, and you will realize how much faster you can recover. Here's the example:

"Well, I was recently fired from my job, and this is going to be quite a change. These people needed more information on what, exactly, I was doing. They managed to concentrate on everything but telling me what I was accountable for. So I'll have a rigorous time paying my bills, and I'll have to come up with some creative way to be able to handle the mortgage. Christmas is going to be light, and I'll have a few challenges figuring out what my next moves are. This is a time for change. It looks like my job was a poor fit in the first place. If I really think about it, I was unhappy much of the time, so actually it looks like it's a good time for a change in my life. I'm going to go out and find a new job that's a much better fit for me. It will just take a while to recover."

You will notice now how you're wiser in reflection and more thoughtful in your bias about what happened. When you speak in inclusion, you create forward movement, and you will see a much faster recovery from your anger.

SUMMARY

The objective is to speak so that you can recover from anger faster and move from problem description to problem solution. Whatever you put into your brain, whether good or bad, is all that your brain has to work with. Your entire being is stimulated by what goes into your mind through your sense organs. A product will emerge from repeating a hateful speech or humming Mozart. If you put angry clichés and hateful thoughts into your mind through books, television, or friends and family, those will result in depressing and pessimistic thoughts and actions in the future. On the other hand, like my friend learning to recognize classical music, if you go to bed listening to Mozart's 21st piano concerto, you may wake up in a wonderful mood with the *allegro*, *andante*, or the *allegro vivace* bouncing around in your head. When you consciously choose to put positive and value-filled items into your world, that's optimism, and that's taking more control of your life.

SMOOTHING OUT THE BUMPS
POINTS TO REMEMBER/THINGS TO DO

1. A small amount of anger can do a lot of damage to your life.

2. If you are repeatedly exposed to something (hostile words or classical music), it will show up in parts of your life.

3. People often express themselves in hostile terms on television, radio, and in person. This can stifle your optimism.

4. Anger is perfectly natural. Express it but notice if you slip into exclusionary or negative patterns.

5. Some depression seems to be connected with unexpressed hostility.

6. It's easy to accuse others, but remember to look at yourself.

7. Exclusionary language is destructive and encourages angry responses in yourself and in others.

8. Inclusionary language focuses on action, problem solution, and recovery from anger.

The Word on Chapter

8

Improving your personal performance may involve spending your efforts on trying less rather than more. Whether it is in athletics, music, public speaking, or sales, you can achieve optimum performance by saying the right things to yourself and to others.

OPTIMUM PERSONAL PERFORMANCE

—

"Whoever controls the language, the images, controls the race."
Allen Ginsberg

As you think about your personal performance in your work, your personal pursuits, or other areas of your life, you may feel that there is a certain amount of untapped potential within you. That's what many people have reported to me—that when they think about their ability to perform well, when they think about their actualized levels of achievement, they almost always mention large areas of untapped potential.

This chapter dives into how you can improve your personal performance by mastering what you think and what you say to others and to yourself.

This mastery comes more easily when we take the advice of Thomas Huxley. This British biologist and writer suggested that we should "sit down before a fact as a little child, be prepared to give up every preconceived notion." As you work through this book and this chapter, be prepared to let go of old ideas that compromise results. Huxley went on to say, "Follow humbly wherever and to whatever abysses nature leads, or you shall learn nothing." Although he was writing this in a letter to Charles Kingsley, we can apply it today for better choices in our language and for improved optimism in life.

When you talk to anybody who performs at an extraordinary level in athletics, music, public speaking, or sales, and you ask what it really takes to reach that level, they will frequently say, "Well, 90 percent of it is mental." Now, if such a large slice of our "effort" pie is mental, it seems reasonable to learn everything we can about how this mental factor is either helped or hindered. If we learn behaviors that assist our mental game, we come out ahead. Also, when we learn to recognize the pitfalls and negative effects of other behaviors, we can gear our lives and our careers in ways that avoid these harmful practices. This chapter and the remaining chapters in this book will assist you in smoothing out more of the bumps you will surely encounter as you progress farther on the road to optimism.

SKATES, MUSIC, SPEECHES, AND MONEY

I will take you through some examples from four general areas of performance: athletics; music; public speaking; and sales. These will serve to show how your language and mental set-up determine how well you will perform. This section will also clarify why performance can take a dramatic nose-dive when you least expect it. Here again, it depends on which road you take as you set the stage for your performance.

ATHLETIC PERFORMANCE

If this cerebral link to performance is accurate, a huge amount of what goes on with you physically is a reflection of your self-talk—the dialogue you engage in with yourself prior to performing.

In 1993, I went to the World Figure Skating Championships. All the top skaters of the day were there. What was interesting was what I saw each skater do during the finals of the women's competition. Everyone fell. That's right. Every one of the top five skaters fell. What was even more fascinating was what happened later, during the evening individual non-competitive exhibition. Not one of the skaters fell!

JUST HAVING A GOOD TIME

When it comes to performance, I am always surprised at how people shoot themselves in the foot. The pressure is enormous for most people to make sure they win, or to make sure they don't lose. There is quite a distinction between winning and not losing—one opens out to potential while the other closes in for protection.

Let's talk a bit more about women's figure skating. In the Women's Figure Skating Finals of the Calgary Winter Olympics, Katarina Witt of the former East Germany and Debbie Thomas of the USA were the favorites going into the finals. Katarina was in second place and Debbie was in first. During her final performance, Debbie tightened up and fell. She received the bronze medal. Katarina skated brilliantly and earned the gold. Do you remember who got the silver? Elizabeth Manley of Canada, who somehow came up from eighth place, out of nowhere, to capture the audience with an extraordinarily magical performance. Afterwards, when asked by the media how she happened to perform so well, she said, "Well, I've had so many disappointments in the past, I thought I would just go out and have a good time."

This tells us that Elizabeth's mental state was critical to her performance. We can only ask, "Could she have performed at this level sooner if her self-talk had given her a more relaxed and positive message?" I have total confidence that better self-talk would have produced the positive results even sooner. Our entire journey down this road is filled with beautiful examples of positive preparation on the optimistic side of things and then resulting thoughts and feelings that support great outcomes and solid performances. Yes, selecting the right words to tell yourself works and each of you has the power to do it.

SOMETIMES IT HURTS FOR REAL!

You will recall Oksana Baiul, the little girl orphan from Russia who at 16 became a world-wide phenomenon at the Winter Olympics in Lillehammer, Norway, in 1994. Prior to the finals she was accidentally skewered in the leg by another skater's blade. She was badly hurt, and it was thought that she would not be able to compete. But she went on the next day to a brilliant performance and eventually won the gold medal. So what went through her mind? You can bet it was less about the pain and bad timing of the accident, and more about impressed judges, an adoring crowd, and wonderful scores. She thought it through in advance.

What is common, if anything, in these performers? What allowed them to rise to these phenomenal achievements? What was their mental state, and what were they always saying to themselves? In all cases, their thought and language were geared to what was presently before them. They seldom focused on what was excluded or other "excuse" material. They also realized how to translate the power of these thoughts and words into actions and even medals.

MUSICAL PERFORMANCE

Music can be a powerful mood-setter when you are the listener. We listen to vigorous, pounding music to put us in the mood to exercise or accomplish a tough task. We put on soft music to create a close, romantic ambiance. At other times we want to reminisce about a wonderful musical, play, or movie we've seen, so we play the soundtrack from *Phantom of the Opera*, *Les Misérables*, or *Amadeus*.

Someone creates (or attempts to create) the beautiful music we enjoy. Many people have reported to me that when they were children, they played an instrument or took music lessons. Maybe you, too, played piano or clarinet or trumpet or some other instrument. If you were like me, you practiced an instrument for many years.

Remember what happened when company came over for dinner? After dinner someone would say, "Oh, Mitchell, get your clarinet and play." You may have said to yourself what I said to myself: "Oh, no. I don't want to play. I won't do it very well." But everyone would encourage me to play, and I would finally relent. I would choose music that I had played during practice many times very successfully. However, now I was worried about how well I would do, and I would tell myself, "Don't mess up. Don't squeak. Don't play the wrong note." And, of course, that's exactly what I did.

A friend of mine played classical guitar in college. He used to get so nervous before performing that he couldn't eat the day of the performance. He played and replayed the most difficult parts of the score. This made him focus on those sections, tighten up, and pluck the wrong string too often. One day he was set to perform a piece called "Sounds of Bells," a difficult and catchy tune that showed a bit of virtuosity. The performance was at 3 p.m. Earlier in the day he simply gave up feeling pressured about the performance. He decided just to play the piece without worry or any more practice. He ended up enjoying his day and breezing through the music. Twenty years later, he still remembers the lesson of letting go, trusting his preparation and optimism, and seeing great results as the audience stood and applauded.

TAXES, SPIDERS, AND PUBLIC SPEAKING

What causes most people more anxiety than anything else? Some may guess taxes, while others would bet money that it's death. Some might think it would be deep water, hairy spiders, or fear of heights. Well, depending on how much of it you do, the answer may or may not surprise you. According to *The Book of Lists*, it is public speaking. In survey after survey, making a public presentation tops the list of the most nerve-wracking, confidence shaking experiences we humans must occasionally endure.

You may share this anxiety. Notice what you say to yourself. "Oh, I couldn't possibly get up their in front of that microphone, in front of all those people. I just couldn't possibly do that. I don't want to look stupid. I don't want to look like a fool." After repeating some of these very same phrases to herself, a woman in a college evening course elected to take a failing grade in the class because she refused to do the final three-minute presentation. In this case the amazed instructor relented and gave her a break. The instructor gained an appreciation for how frightening public speaking can be for some. He assigned her an additional written project and gave her a passing grade.

SPEAKING . . . AND YOUR CAR?

It would be great if speaking in public were like driving a car. When you are driving, do you really think about it or do you just do it? You just do it, of course. Many times when you're driving, after several miles you just sort of wake up with a feeling of surprise that you've stayed on the road. It's as if you were in another world and not paying attention to the driving. You were really thinking about something else. Well, what is your mental state when it comes to driving a car? You just do it with a quantum leap of trust. Your mental language, or self-talk, about driving says that you are going to be fine and that your driving performance will be successful. And almost always your driving is fine.

Which actually holds more potential for danger, driving a car or public speaking? Yet our self-talk when it comes to public speaking, the far less dangerous activity, creates considerably more anxiety. What we believe when driving a car is, "I will be fine." What we say to ourselves when public speaking is, "Don't be a fool."

DO'S AND DON'TS OF YOUR MIND

Some people dream in living color, while others can barely recall a fuzzy black-and-white image of the past night's drama. As the day progresses, the details and images of our dreams often fade. This may be a stretch for many of us, but like the fading details of our dreams, our mind has difficulty remembering whether an admonition started with a "do" or a "don't." Therefore, if I say, "Don't look like a fool," then I may translate it into being overly concerned and end up actually looking like a fool. On the other hand, if I say, "I will be fine driving this car," then I usually will be just fine (of course the other guy may have a slight "vision" problem).

It is curious that although the mind has difficulty differentiating between "do" and "don't," our self-talk prior to performing is in some form of "don't." We often say or think things like, "Don't tighten up, don't look stupid, don't blow it, don't lose voice control."

It appears that the same kind of language does harm in sports, music, and in giving speeches. It's the language of exclusion: "Don't blow it. Don't tighten up. Don't look stupid." Let's look at our final area for this chapter and see if language and mental set-up play as important a role in sales performance.

SALES PERFORMANCE

For a lot of us, being in a selling mode creates anxiety. Why? Because there is the threat of failure and rejection if someone refuses to buy. We are hoping our prospects will buy, and the closer it gets to the wire, the more anxious we become. That's why so many people in sales have the biggest problem with closing.

When I do training in sales, the topic that most of the audience is highly interested in is closing. Closing the sale is the moment of truth when the prospects will buy or decide to postpone. The threat of rejection is so big at this point that most salespeople resist even asking the closing question. They stall. What are we saying to ourselves when we stall? What is the language we're using that causes hysteria?

We often say, "Now, don't push. Don't let this customer go away. Don't allow him or her to say no." Predictably, we tighten up; unknowingly, we encourage, even force, the potential buyer to resist. We never ask the question, and then the buyer is never confronted with having to buy.

FAKE IT 'TIL YOU MAKE IT

Many people register disgust or at least displeasure when they hear the cliché, "fake it 'til you make it." It sounds too much like hype or hard selling. A closer look uncovers a mental competitive edge worth considering. Assuming basic ethics and integrity, we can take the saying to mean we should assume the confidence and competence needed to get the job done. If 90% of stellar performance is mental, this will help us control that portion of the equation. Confident salespeople sell more. Salespeople who assume they are competent do the things that equate to competence—they study, ask, learn, practice. What they don't do is make excuses about what is not there or what is missing. So "fake it 'til you make it" has some very strong positives. The opposite would be "excuse it 'til you lose it."

SELLING SKILLS AND A GOLF BALL

Let's try golf. If you play golf, you will know exactly what I'm talking about. Let's say you're at the first tee and looking 350 yards straight down the fairway. Off to the right is a pond of water. You're about to tee off and all you have to do is hit the ball straight down the fairway. It's very easy. Or is it? What do you say to yourself at this time? What is your self-talk when you get up to the ball and you're about to hit it? Do you say to yourself, "All I'm going to do is hit it straight down the fairway"? Do you say that? No. You know exactly what you say. You say to yourself over and over, "Don't hit that ball in the water. Don't even look at the water. Don't let the water bother you and don't be stupid and don't tighten up because you know you always tighten up. And don't slice it because you always slice it. You know how you are. You always slice it. Don't slice it. And don't let your golf partners bother you or distract you. There is nothing to be concerned about here, so don't tighten up, don't let the water bother you, don't even look at the water, and don't slice it."

So you finally fire that ball out there, and where does it go? Well, into the water; right on schedule. Then what do you say to yourself? You say, "I knew it!"

Let's suppose you hit the ball great, and it goes right down the middle of the fairway and lands perfectly. Very often at that point what you will say is, "Boy, where did that come from?" Or, at most, you give yourself some exclusionary feedback and say, "Not bad."

A DANCING EXAMPLE AND SELF-TALK

Let's go to dancing. Notice how you are when it comes to dancing. Many people are reluctant to dance because they think that they dance improperly. They think they are going to be noticed by everyone. Imagine that you are attending a dance at a local community hall. It's a sit-down dinner dance and the dress is semiformal. There are about 500 people attending, all dressed up, many of whom are your friends and people of the same position in the community. Everyone is drinking and eating and talking. The dinner is over, the after-dinner speeches are completed, and the band now begins to play. Do you immediately get on the dance floor with your partner? Do you race out onto the floor and enjoy the dance? I doubt it. No. I imagine that you wait for the dance floor to fill up. Then you won't feel self-conscious. Just to take the edge off, you might have another drink to give yourself confidence.

What's the deal? What's the big problem with dancing? I've asked this question of many people over the years and most of them say the same thing: "I don't dance very well. I don't remember the steps. I'm afraid I won't look right. I look silly. I'm self-conscious.

Everyone will be looking at me. I would look pretty stupid. I don't know how to dance."

WHAT'S THE REAL PROBLEM?

What is the real problem here? Clearly, it is the concern that you will look inept on the dance floor. Everyone will be staring at you. Everyone will criticize you or disapprove or laugh or think poorly of you.

Suppose you do go out on the dance floor, and you and your partner are the only ones out there. Suppose some people are looking at you. Are you ever going to find out what they think? Are you going to take a survey after your performance? Are you going to go up to them and say, "Excuse me, I was just on the dance floor and, of course, you were looking at me, and I'm taking a poll. Just exactly how well did I do?" Have you ever had anyone, yell out at you while you were dancing, "Oh, you meatball! Do yourself a favor and get off the dance floor. You look ridiculous." Has that ever happened? Pretty unlikely.

Your anxiety on the dance floor is really unnecessary. Your anxiety, again, is a reflection of self-talk. We're back to the Behavior Triangle: What you say affects how you feel, which affects how you think, and vice versa. If you feel anxiety, you are probably responding to self-talk that goes something like this, "Don't be stupid. You don't dance right. You don't know what you're doing. You don't want everybody looking at you."

Why do people dance in the first place? Think about it. To have fun, of course. Yet you, with your fear of looking stupid, are reluctant to go out on the dance floor to do something that would certainly be fun because you fear something that you will never find out about.

Consider that the feelings of concern that you have on the dance floor, the feelings of anxiety, are the same feelings that you may have in sales, are the same feelings that you may have in public speaking, are the same feelings that you may have in golf, are the same that you have in any kind of competition or performance. *All the anxiety is over fear of failure, fear of loss, fear of rejection, fear of looking stupid, and fear of tightening up.*

YOUR SELF-TALK IS PLAYING

Most of successful performance is based on your mental preparation leading up to the event and your mental state while you are in the process of performing. You can say that the performance begins well in advance of the actual act or the steps it takes to complete the task. Your mind engages long before your body or your briefcase go through the motions. Going back to the dance floor, ask yourself what kind of language you use on yourself when you're experiencing the feelings of concern or anxiety? Chances are very good that your language is one that amplifies the fear. That's right, the language of exclusion. Here are examples of this very kind of self-talk as it happens in relation to performance:

- "I hope I don't choke."
- "Don't tighten up."
- "Don't let those people who are watching bother you."
- "Don't hit it in the water."
- "Don't embarrass yourself."
- "Don't look stupid."
- "You know you can't do it."

- "Why didn't you do that right?"
- "Don't think about it."
- "You're not concentrating."

All of these self-talk remarks are in the language of exclusion. Notice how often your self-talk is an endless tape playing over and over and over again conditioning your mind to respond accordingly. It is the language of exclusion; it is essentially talking about what is missing; it is talking in deficits, making you pessimistic, negative, and compromising your performance.

What would happen to you and your performance if you simply changed your language to one of inclusion? Just suppose you decided to deal with every kind of performance by using a language that would actually help you stay optimistic, with a language that affected the Behavior Triangle in such a way that your feelings and thoughts helped you to perform in an optimal way. What might happen?

Let's suppose you use these kinds of remarks:

- "Hit it down the fairway."
- "I hope I do well."
- "Relax and let yourself focus."
- "Just focus on only what you're doing."
- "You can do it."
- "You look fine."
- "Think about this point—the one you are playing."
- "Be a winner and concentrate."
- "You're going to be able to do it."

Is it difficult to give yourself permission to say these kinds of things? Make a practice of reading these examples out loud over and over and over; then watch what happens to your outlook. You'll be quite surprised to see a difference in your attitude and your performance.

SUMMARY

When it comes to optimum performance, top performers in every dimension of life have a mental state that is different from others. Their mental state is almost always a reflection of an internal dialogue that is playing all the time. They use self-talk that allows their Behavior Triangle to create a performance result that is optimum.

I have found that exclusionary language is omnipresent when it comes to performance and that your mind will follow exactly what you are focusing on. If you say, "Don't get upset," then, of course, you are focusing on being upset. The mind, remember, has a huge problem differentiating between "do" and "don't." I recommend that you practice the language of inclusion, which will help you focus on what you want to do and help you to avoid what you're trying to not do.

The language of inclusion allows you to concentrate on what you want to achieve rather than trying to stop doing what you don't want to achieve. At the beginning of this chapter we discussed Thomas Huxley's advice on observing facts as a child and giving up preconceived notions in order to learn new skills. I encourage you to be that *learning child* when faced with new information and to speak the language of inclusion in your self-talk. This will affect your Behavior Triangle and your optimism, which will increase your performance across the board.

SMOOTHING THE ROAD
POINTS TO REMEMBER/THINGS TO DO

1. Be open to new facts and techniques. There is always a way to do something better.

2. Superior athletic performance is largely mental.

3. Outstanding musical performance is largely mental.

4. Excellent pubic speaking performance is largely mental.

5. Exemplary sales performance is largely mental.

6. Remember your skill base, discipline, and rigor. These always play a role in optimum performance.

7. Your prospects are better when you focus on *winning* rather than on *not losing*.

8. Up to 90% of successful performance is based on your mental preparation (before) and your mental state (during) your performance.

9. Use the Language of Inclusion in your self-talk.

The Word on Chapter

9

*We take risks with relationships and partnerships.
Both are unions of forces with a goal or aim in mind.
This chapter distills ways of improving relationships
with your language choices and good old common sense.*

RISK TAKING &
RELATIONSHIPS

—

The year was 1950, and in his Nobel Prize acceptance
speech, William Faulkner said, "I believe that man will
not merely endure; he will prevail. He is immortal, not
because he alone among creatures has an inexhaustible
voice, but because he has a soul, a spirit capable of
compassion and sacrifice and endurance."

These words speak of the uniqueness of the human
race. A half century after he spoke them, they make us

pause and wonder what really makes us human. This voice and soul and spirit Faulkner spoke of gather much of their strength from association with others. Alone, they yield little until others share their meaning. My belief is that this immortality is heated by relationships that mold that voice, soul, and spirit, and forges character—it is this immersion in various relationships that sets some on the path of negativism and others on the road toward optimism.

When we examine the human condition we see a series of relationships. Whether it's at the intensely personal level or on a worldwide commercial scale, all that is important depends on relationships. It also seems that all human achievement that endures owes a small debt for its durability to nourished relationships.

When relationships are strong and respectful, people will be forgiving of each other when they make mistakes or when they drop the ball. But when relationships are strained or based on a foundation of mistrust, people become hypersensitive and often get defensive in any situation that looks like a threat.

One of the actions I speak of in my audio cassette series, the *Ten Perry Commitments*, is *Commitment: Engage The Power Of Relationships*. You do this by first demonstrating trust. This demonstration of trust is like tuning your car. When you pick your car up from the mechanic and drive off, all major systems are synchronized and timed to run efficiently. *Relationship tuning* happens when everyone integrates their contributions and skills. It's "you and me," and the output, like a well-tuned auto, is more than the sum of the parts. This trust, especially in relationships, involves some uncertainty. It's not always easy. But the benefit is that these types of risks pay handsome dividends.

THE RISK OF RELATIONSHIPS

Any risk involves the possibility of loss. Many endeavors can be highly leveraged by adding an appropriate amount of risk in a planned and strategic fashion. In financial investing, your choices range from simply protecting the money you already have, all the way to aggressively investing in highly volatile and risky endeavors. When the risk factor is greater, your potential for a high return is greater, too (although so is the possibility of loss).

Another area where the addition of risk is most crucial to increased success is in the creative arts. Whether their field be dance, painting, or music, artists who rise to the top know how to take the risks they need in order to stand out and receive the reviews from critics that send them soaring. Here again, they still sometimes fail. That is the nature of taking a risk.

QUITE A CONTRAST!

We can build incredible buildings that reach to the sky—yet we destroy them through war or terror campaigns. We can use biotechnology that increases life expectancy and the quality of life—yet we are burdened with the task of dismantling and destroying biological weapons developed for use against other human beings. We can create global telecommunications so that multiple populations can interact with each other simultaneously—yet we fear and mistrust other cultures.

There is a great confidence that we have the skills to reach lofty goals, but something gets in the way of the application of those skills to construct enduring partnerships. Let's go back to Roman times for a quick example.

A HORSE FOR SENATOR?

Caligula, one of the twelve Caesars of the Roman Empire during the first century AD., either never believed in relationships or lost faith in the partnership between himself and the leaders of the day. He rose to the top of the ranks by skill, cunning, and deceit. Once, in order to humiliate the senators of Rome, he actually appointed his own horse to the senate. This is a potent example of how masterful potential for success sometimes mixes with astounding ineptitude in relationships. The result is a downward spiral. Of course, history, and this anecdote of his horse in the senate, tell us that Caligula was crazy, but don't we sometimes see this paradox in ourselves and those around us today? We build on our goals and risk failure only to trample on our work with our methods. In our times, we may not read about horses or golden retrievers being appointed to corporate boards but we still see and experience unusual behavior, like Caligula's, that destroys relationships.

Perhaps our relationships would hold up better if we nudged them down a path of optimism. By this I mean doing what we can to recognize and transmit useful and helpful information more often than passing along useless and harmful messages. All the data is not in on what exactly makes relationships work, but we can trust our intuition. Do you remember the French philosopher Blaise Pascal and his famous Pascalian bet? Writing for the religious and nonreligious of his day, he reasoned if you refuse to believe in God you lose, regardless of the outcome. Your disbelief disqualifies you for any future benefits of paradise whether it exists or not—you can only win by buying a ticket. If you do believe and God doesn't exist, you lose nothing.   On the other hand, if you do believe in God and he (or she) exists, you win everything—that is Pascal's bet.   If we remove the religious overtones and replace them with optimistic language, Pascal might agree that trusting in the power of optimistic language will most likely result in better partnerships and multi-faceted relationships. If you refuse to believe that better language choices help relationships, you probably will resist using more positive, action-oriented, inclusionary language. Whether it works or not is irrelevant.   Now, even if you're yet to be convinced (I'll keep working on you— you keep reading!) but you give it a chance, you are allowing for the possibility of reaping some of the benefits. Pascal would be pleased.

We tend to be destructive beings. Our relationships suffer from this unhealthy habit. We also lose any leverage for building and growing when we tear our relationships apart.   But despite our sometimes destructive tendencies, we can, and often do, prevail with acts of caring, respect, repair, and maturity. Something causes our strength and character to shine through amidst all the negativity, doubt, hostility, and cynicism. My opinion is that our initial sense of optimism and our language choices that support optimism allow the "good stuff" to shine through.

APPRECIATING THE GOOD STUFF

Many of you are chagrined that you seem to require a crisis to get your act together. You ask yourself, "What will it take for me to learn?" The unfaithful spouse or lover gets caught in a lie. The boss makes impossible promises to employees, and when she can't deliver, the staff quits. The professional works himself to exhaustion and falls ill, missing important deadlines. The question you want to ask yourself now is: Do we as a species have to continue to be dependent upon crises for us to change our behavior? Is it possible that we could have evolved to the point where we could change our behavior in advance of having a crisis? And what about the planet? What do we do now? Will we need a global crisis again to get our attention? Do we really have to have a huge pile of bad news for us to become more socially responsible, for us to contribute more value to society and to become more "givers" as opposed to "consumers?" I am much more hopeful than this. There are ways to get over this selfish and shortsighted pattern.

HOW DO WE OVERCOME?

Whether it's dealing with international conflict or dealing with our own family problems, we generally make things worse before we make things better. So what are our alternatives? Can we really overcome our primitive tendencies? Can we really learn from our mistakes? Can we prevent reinventing the wheel with every generation? Can we actually become mature enough to step up to the plate and be real grown-ups without a crisis? Can we really become smarter, more mature, and more squared away? Can we really overcome our issues of race and fear and condemnation when people are different from us?

I'm convinced that we can. However, we find it very difficult just to change our minds. It's important that we have some kind of a tool that allows us to actually change our behavior on a regular basis. When we think pessimistically, we tend to get more paranoid. When we are pessimistic and we look at the down side and we focus on what is missing on a regular basis, we are going to become more defensive, more suspicious, and more hostile. In estranging ourselves from one another we become more condemning and critical in proportion to how afraid we become.

Our language of exclusion contributes to this escalating pessimism. People can make wholesale changes in the nature of their relationships by changing their own behavior. But, as we've covered in earlier chapters, in order to change your own behavior, you need to have at your fingertips a skill that allows you to really change the nature of how you think, which affects how you feel. Remember the interplay of the Behavior Triangle's *say-think-feel*!

I've spent much time working with many people from every continent, many of whom speak multiple languages. In most of the languages that I've encountered, people have the same propensity to speak in exclusion. In Spanish they say, "de nada;" in French they say, "Il n'ya pas de quoi;" in British English they say, "it was nothing, not at all;" in Italian they say, "no problemo." Most of the adults around the world seem to speak about what is not there. As you have learned, this is speaking in exclusion. And like that Pascalian bet we discussed earlier, it is risky to speak this way. We'll have more detail on this in the next chapter.

MARRIAGE RELATIONS

For our discussion, here are a few of the possible risks involved with marriage:

- Mate selection—making the proper initial selection of the person who matches you in important areas.
- Permanency—it's supposed to be forever or at least a long time.
- Mutual growth—how will you change together and communicate with each other about your growth?
- Opportunity cost—other options are either minimized or eliminated.

Having treated just about every kind of marital problem you can imagine in my private practice, I became aware of some very common problems in marriages. One is that the very qualities that you're attracted to in a mate in the beginning phases of a relationship can become irritating as the years go by. People in marriages have communication problems, and one of the contributors is the fact that both parties often speak in ways that accentuate the negative and focus on missing elements of the relationship.

If you want to keep your marriage healthy and lasting, nourish it with a series of behaviors and communication styles that help the relationship stay healthy. If you speak in exclusion, then you are focusing on what is missing in your relationship. When you think about your marriage and when you talk to your partner, you might make remarks like this:

- "You're not meeting my needs."
- "You don't really understand me like you should."
- "You're not clean enough."
- "You're not sexy enough."
- "You don't take good enough care of yourself."

- "You're not being responsive to me."
- "You're not listening to me."

Most of the time married couples point out what isn't there, either in themselves or in their partner. I asked couples to point out to each other regularly what they really liked about each other—one partner spending a couple of minutes telling the other partner what he or she really liked about the other. It was pleasing to note that much of the severity of the problems softened. They changed from what was missing to what was there. This led to a lessening of the risks that we opened with at the beginning of this section.

When you practice speaking in inclusion, you're much more likely to talk about your mate in terms of what is there and what is appreciated, as opposed to what is missing and, therefore, is a source of unhappiness. Speaking in inclusion allows you to realize what exists in your marriage as opposed to what is the deficit; it allows you to solve problems more than describe them. This leads you to take more responsibility for changing things rather than to highlight what is missing in your partner.

FAMILY RELATIONS

In family matters we see many similarities to the marriage relationship. Here we add and substitute other risk areas to the list:

- Cohesiveness—can the family stick together as members grow and evolve?
- Group enjoyment—doing things that most members will enjoy and find pleasurable.
- Values—defining and displaying values that are accepted and adopted.

- Safety—within and outside of the home.
- Education—based on school location, funds, and motivation.

Community leaders regularly exhort that the breakdown of the American family has been causing enormous problems in society. It is true that as families break down, as one-parent families increase, and as more fathers are absent, we will see a further breakdown with a ripple effect throughout our communities.

Families spend too much time criticizing, condemning, and estranging themselves from each other. Here again we find people talking about what is not there in their family as opposed to what is there:

- There's not enough love.
- There's not enough involvement.
- Dad is never home.
- Mom doesn't seem to care.
- The children aren't doing well in school.

Speaking in inclusion allows for an optimistic explanatory style. It is much more likely to permit people to capitalize on their family strengths as opposed to compensating for what is missing. This minimizes some of the risks involved in the family setting.

RACE RELATIONS

Race relations in the United States seems to be a type of ping-pong issue where different sides claim similar attributes for their own group (tolerance, fairness, open mindedness) and they assign contrasting characteristics to other groups of people (intolerance, unfairness, closed mindedness). The majority in most racial groups work on personal awareness and attempt to practice tolerance. Unfortunately, some members of all sides blame their trials and defeats on members of other groups. They proceed to lob grenades over into the other group and predict a racism-tainted response.

Some of the risks in this category have played themselves out far too many times:

- Smoldering hatred—disgust for other groups that goes unexplored and unimproved.
- Active hate events—rallies, protests, church burnings, and bodily harm.
- Discrimination—treating people differently based solely on their race rather than on skills or talents.
- Ethnic pride—at the expense of others or in the form of private jokes or ostracism of group members who mingle outside of the group.

From listening to the people in the media, it seems that fingers are always being pointed at each other, that blaming continues, and that plenty of energy is expended by everyone condemning one another rather than thinking of a way to get along. This maximizes the risks listed above.

One way to look at race relations is to always be in a problem description mode. The problem is "them"—the Blacks, the Whites, the Hispanics, the Jews—"they" are the problem, whoever "they" are. No matter which group you're in, if you're in this blaming mode, it is very likely that you have a language of exclusion:

- "They don't allow us opportunities."
- "They are not aware of what we go through."

- "Nobody knows the pain that we have suffered."
- "It isn't fair. I didn't cause this problem. Can't they just get over it?"

What's interesting is that one of the ways in which you ensure the likelihood of a real change in race relations is to get people to change their behavior. Look at the Behavior Triangle: What you say affects how you feel, which affects how you think. This may be a start. On a talk show regarding race, there was one gentleman who said one-quarter of all black males in this country are either in prison or on drugs. This means that 25 percent of black males in this country are not contributing members of society. However, another gentleman pointed out that while this is a problem, it's important to remember that three-quarters of black males are contributing members of society. That is a perfect illustration of how the language of inclusion has much more of a healing effect than exclusion.

SOCIAL RELATIONS

If you turn on any television talk show these days, it seems that all are exposing the unattractive parts of American society. They are almost always problem description shows or "victim of the week" displays. The spectacle delves into who is the most mistreated, who is the most depressed, or who are the most misunderstood members of society. Rarely do they ever solve problems; instead, they describe them. If you watch even casually, you will note that guests are laying the groundwork for perpetual misery. They seem negative and pessimistic. Most refuse to take responsibility for their desperate or depraved circumstances, and almost all revel in being victims. This lays the groundwork for turbulent social issues to fester and explode without a skilled populace ready to take the reins and permanently solve the issues. The risks involved in our social relations include:

- Entitlement mentality—everyone deserves everything (see the chapter on paying dues).
- One-upmanship—stressing the extreme negativity of their particular case.
- Setting an example—children and young adults accept this as the normal method of communication.
- Isolation—normal and responsible people will avoid contact with abusers who focus on the absence of their benefits.

The nature of what is being shown on television reflects our social patterns just as advertising is a reflection of what people buy. Our public and social distractions and entertainment mimic the wholesome and uplifting side and the tawdry underbelly of American society. Many feel that these images show deteriorating standards in our culture.

Imagine what would happen if just a critical few people started speaking in inclusion. It could be contagious! Pessimism would gradually change to optimism and people would take more personal responsibility for themselves and the circumstances around them. The talk shows might be forced to switch to educational or nature documentaries. Many letters-to-the-editor would become less angry and constipated in favor of positive accounts of good deeds and positive activities in the neighborhoods and communities. One editor says she receives nine negative or politically biased letters-to-the-editor for each positive letter that someone takes the time to write.

It would be refreshing to see a shift in the balance of pessimism and optimism. Rather than saying, "I don't know," people would say, "I'm going to find out." Instead of saying, "I can't do anything about this," people would say, "I'm going to learn how to do something about this." The nature of social relations in this country would change dramatically.

SUMMARY

It may be that Faulkner's spirit of "compassion and sacrifice and endurance" takes root when our personal, social, and global lives focus on the words that nudge our actions towards the *up* side—the *optimistic* side. It may be risky to take some of the advice in this chapter. But it may be even riskier *not* to take it. As you continue progressing along this road, consider which option includes more danger: The path you have been following that may include more negativity and pessimism or a path with road markers and signs that direct your language and your feelings and your thoughts to optimism. I think I know which one you will choose!

SMOOTHING OUT THE BUMPS
POINTS TO REMEMBER/THINGS TO DO

1. Relationships make the world go 'round. Take time to learn how they work.

2. The right amount of risk adds leverage to your efforts.

3. Be aware that some of your actions can destroy good relationships without you even knowing it.

4. Change your behavior before the crisis. Learn what you can control and be proactive in changing your behavior.

5. The *Pascalian* bet suggests that you bet on the good side of an issue when betting on the other side will ensure that you get nothing.

6. Marriage relations improve when each person talks about what they like about the other—simple but effective inclusionary speech.

7. Families can also benefit by substituting inclusionary language whenever possible.

8. Racial groups will be less polarized as forward-thinking members build on recent progress and the goodwill of the vast majority who want relations to improve.

9. Our social and entertainment outlets mold society. Social relations will reflect the style and content of what's printed or broadcast—exclusionary begets exclusionary unless someone speaks up.

10. Change your language to inclusion and watch relationships change for the better.

The Word on Chapter

10

*She says "yes"—They say "no"—We say "maybe"—
He says "perhaps!" There is good and bad in most of
the choices we make. Every choice carries a
consequence.*

RISK TAKING:
INCLUSION VS. EXCLUSION

—

*"I would define, in brief, the poetry of words as the
rhythmical creation of Beauty."*
Edgar Allan Poe

Gerald, a middle-aged business owner, hears a knock
on his door. He opens it and finds Sylvia, a law student
and friend. She has offered to give him a ride to the
airport for his trip to Germany. The two friends greet
each other, load his bags into the car, and head out to the

airport. On the way, their conversation goes something like this:

> *Sylvia*: "Gerald, you have one hell of a lifestyle. You're really lucky."
>
> *Gerald*: "Yeah, but I've got so much to do. I don't know if I should be taking this trip. I haven't finished a couple of proposals."
>
> *Sylvia*: "Oh, you'll finish it all when you get back. I think you've got the best lifestyle of anyone I know."
>
> *Gerald*: "Hum, I guess I'm pretty lucky, but I've worked hard. In fact, I'm in the middle of projects with two large corporations and a local city government. I don't know how I'll get them done."
>
> *Sylvia*: "Every one of my friends and law school classmates have loads to do, and so what! You seem to add great stuff to your life, stuff that anyone could do if they wanted to, but you just make it a priority and it works. It's a real blessing. You should be more thankful."
>
> *Gerald*: "Do you really think so, Sylvia? I guess everything I've worked for has come through and I'm living the lifestyle I set out as a goal over ten years ago. Wow, you're right. I should count my blessings."
>
> *Sylvia*: "Here we are. Got your passport? Have a great vacation!"

This interchange highlights many of the principles of the Language Inclusion Process we have explored in the earlier chapters of this book. It also shows that there are clearly some liabilities to speaking in exclusion or always focusing on what's missing in life or work.

This chapter presents liabilities, or risks, of speaking in exclusion and some of the many corresponding benefits of speaking in inclusion. If you speak the bulk of the time in exclusion or are speaking about what is missing, speaking about what is not there, it means that you have compromised your potential to work at an optimal level. As in our story, these risks contribute significantly to pessimism and a pessimistic explanatory style. But as we saw with Gerald, there is hope that we can recognize what we are doing and then proceed to adjust our frame of reference.

RISK ONE: EXCLUSION MEANS YOU TALK A LOT

Exclusion requires an awful lot of dialogue. To talk about what is missing, you have to have a long list of possibilities. You have to speak a lot. For example, if I have a cup of coffee in front of me, I can tell you what it is in six words—This is a cup of coffee.

However, the need to tell you about what it is in exclusion requires me to speak a lot. It requires that I say, "It is not this pen, and it is not this paper, and it is not this radio, and it's not this tape recorder, and it's not this lamp." Our language gets some of its flair and flavor by allowing many different ways of expressing ourselves. This, however, seems to be insignificant.

People who can quickly and succinctly home in on an issue are respected. They are trusted to deal clearly and fairly with issues. When we are respected, we make gradual improvements in our self-esteem and our self-concept. These intensely personal aspects of our nature are keys to determining our explanatory style or our enlivened attitude. Volumes of verbiage are a clear sign of an unprepared or cluttered mind. When we use too many words to describe events or feelings, we lose the impact. In our personal and business affairs, it's difficult to make a quick recovery when we've lost the other party by burying them with unfriendly words. Remember, many people are inundated with negatives and pessimistic ways of describing things. They may make it a point to shut it off as soon as possible.

RISK TWO: EXCLUSION MEANS YOU COMPLAIN A LOT

Exclusion increases the amount of complaining. Because you're almost always talking about what's missing, you are constantly describing problems. It's like sitting in the emergency waiting room with an injury. Every time you think your turn is close, someone arrives with a bigger, nastier, and more urgent injury than yours. In this environment everyone is hurt and needs some attention based on a problem. If you have ever had a close friend in the medical profession, you know of the coping mechanisms he or she must use to survive. They control caring deeply for each individual case. They resist being impressed by your pain or your injury. At times, it becomes difficult to sympathize or empathize with you. They have another patient to care for or to worry about.

They may not tell you, but people get very tired of listening to whining and complaining. Perhaps it's our social skills or communication abilities, but we have a tough time telling others to slow down on the complaining because it's driving us crazy. Instead we sit there and listen patiently until we're with someone else who will listen to us complain about what we had to endure with all that complaining. Word gets around that certain folks are never happy, always hurt, and they will tell others about it in minute detail.

RISK THREE: YOU BLAME A LOT

The third liability is that the language of exclusion lets you abdicate responsibility for yourself. It encourages the victim mentality. This is similar to offices where the measurement yardstick is flawed and politics are the method of choice for getting promotions and raises. In this environment some will instantly lay out a plan to blame others for anything that might go wrong.

A buddy of mine named Carl worked at a large high-technology company. His department was one of the first to be equipped with IBM personal computers. Bernard, an internal consultant, was assigned to set up the systems and train the employees. Everything seemed to go wrong as Bernard tried to work in Carl's department and set up the system during an intense manufacturing crunch. People in Carl's department simply were unavailable—it was a tough situation for everyone involved. When pressed by the plant manager, Bernard immediately blamed my friend, Carl, for every part of the problem and delay. Bernard rattled off a list of items that Carl had not done which kept him from completing the project. The plant manager took Carl aside and said that he understood the situation and that he saw that Bernard seemed to be a complainer who easily passed the blame. The manager recommended that Carl meet the manufacturing priorities to the letter, but to get on to the computer project as soon as possible. Carl knew that his boss understood his situation, but after the blaming incident, he had a tough time sitting in meetings with Bernard and taking him seriously.

Some folks seem to search for ways in which they can abdicate responsibility. They constantly talk about the ugly details of the problem and how the beast is bigger than they are. Maybe their problem seems so huge because by speaking in exclusion, they've had to go overboard in describing it.

Taking responsibility for yourself is one of the most important things you can do. Most of the time, it appears, people would much prefer to lift up their finger and point it at somebody, as the consultant did to my friend in the above example. The proliferation of lawsuits in the United States reflects our need to blame someone else and get easy, unearned money rather than to take responsibility for our own behavior.

The language of exclusion seduces you into thinking that a problem about which you are complaining is so big that it dwarfs you and your ability to do anything about it. The tendency to feel defeated before you start looms large. Exclusion may be part of what encourages you to abdicate your responsibility and blame someone else.

To summarize the risks of exclusion:

- You have to talk a lot. The amount of dialogue is enormous.
- You are constantly focused on describing problems and making complaints.
- You get to abdicate responsibility for yourself and really encourage that victim mentality.

How about a breath of fresh air. That was a pretty negative section. I hope you hung in there and picked up some useful information. The reality is that we need to have those types of discussions. They help us to correctly frame the good stuff and recognize it when we see it.

You'll run into more information in later chapters—losing, bad news, paying dues—that seems to be negative but actually goes a long way in supporting your progress down this optimistic road. You're doing well. You've made it through a lot of the book. I encourage you to press on and explore some fascinating ideas for your journey. Let's take a look at some of the benefits of using what we've been discussing in so many chapters.

BENEFIT ONE: INCLUSION MEANS LESS TALK, MORE CLARITY

Max Wertheimer, one of the early, distinguished psychologists, said, "Productive thinking is straight from the heart of the thinker to the heart of the problem." This is one of those statements filled with wisdom and imbued with ageless simplicity. It reminds me of those clock-stopping instances where a child blurts out some taboo conclusion or naked truth—"Why is your nose so big?"—"You're fat!"—"I don't want Uncle Rick to eat with us."—"Grandma smells funny!" Some things just cut to the quick! The reason Wertheimer's quote hits home is because, like the innocent child speaking the truth, it sets a standard of purity in thought and action. It matches what Ernest Hemingway said about his book, *The Old Man And The Sea*. In his reply to a reporter's question about the content of the book, he said that there was not one extra or unnecessary word in the entire manuscript. They began filming the movie shortly thereafter.

The first benefit is that when you speak about clear, present issues, you have to talk less. Your ability to cut out the fluff and the useless dialogue is enhanced. You can reduce the amount of useless chatter and get to the very specific issue or subject matter in an instant. Therefore, by design, when you're talking about what is, you have to describe less and you really summarize the situation quickly. If you're interested in having less dialogue and getting to faster conclusions, you want to talk about things that are there, and do-able and fix-able, which means you quickly get to the heart of the matter.

BENEFIT TWO: INCLUSION MEANS YOU SOLVE PROBLEMS

When you're talking about what is present, when the bulk of your dialogue is in inclusion, you're capitalizing on a real issue as opposed to compensating for some phantom ghost of a missing benefit or entitlement. You're talking about existence as opposed to absence. You are increasing the likelihood of solving the problem. In our office, we often find ourselves squeezed for time and caught between compelling priorities. During these pressing times, we find that when we speak in inclusion our first impulse seems to be to solve problems, simply because we're talking about what's in existence as opposed to what's missing. It's interesting how much more powerful and strong we all feel, more prepared to actually do something about situations. This eliminates the time it takes to translate something that is vague (and usually somewhat uncomfortable) and out of reach into something that has shape and form—an agreement, a proposal, a postponement. This saves us time and confusion.

One of the most popular human resource ideas that was promoted in business in the early 1990s was the concept of empowerment. Empowerment is a condition where people really do feel enabled to do something about their own futures in their own companies. It seems reasonable that if you give people the background information and teach them the process for making decisions, those closest to the issue can make the best choices concerning that issue. The idea was that the more proactive people are in the business, the more results they're going to get. This idea has spread into various versions of work groups, self-managed teams, matrix management, and the virtual office.

While the idea of empowerment certainly makes sense, one of the key questions is: How do you actually create this sense of empowerment? One way is to increase the likelihood that people speak in productive and useful terms. These language choices have an uplifting effect on co-workers rather than the cynical, downer language used all too often. When people use language that inspires, they're going to be talking more about solving problems in less time. Problem solving is a cornerstone of empowerment.

BENEFIT THREE: INCLUSION MEANS YOU TAKE RESPONSIBILITY

Sometimes taking responsibility means taking the heat as well. The good news is that when you're in the hot seat of responsibility often enough, it becomes more and more tolerable. Here's an example from training public speakers. Good instructors who specialize in teaching public speaking or presentation skills often suggest that their students volunteer to speak at every opportunity, in other words, get on the hot seat. They say to always make use of speaking opportunities that require you to get nervous and maybe risk embarrassing yourself. They're joking a bit with that last part, but the idea is sound. When students actually take this bull by the horns, their progress is astounding. Some instructors help the idea sink in by choosing as classroom volunteers the students who look down or away the most. In other words, those trying to avoid volunteering will be selected to be the first ones to make their presentations to the group. Some of these same lessons apply in changing our language.

The third benefit to the Language Inclusion Process is that you begin to take far more responsibility for yourself. You commence to take more positive action. Because you're taking inventory of what's there, then you actually feel more enabled. When you feel more in charge, you're increasingly likely to take action on what you're talking about. There's much more of a tendency or likelihood to take the initiative. You're apt to take ownership for your feelings, take ownership for your actions, take ownership for moving ahead, simply because you're capitalizing on pieces of the puzzle of your own optimism and success that you can see and touch and move around.

SUMMARY

You'll recall the risks of the exclusion habit are that it makes you talk more, complain more, excuse more, and abdicate your responsibility. The benefits to the inclusion process are that you get to talk less, solve more, and take more responsibility for yourself. The gradual shift from exclusion to inclusion enables a step-by-step adoption of an optimistic explanatory style and clearly shows you the road to optimism. You've come a long way with this book and down this road. Keep reading for more valuable information that can change your life.

POSTSCRIPT:

Following his vacation, Gerald calls his friend Sylvia to thank her for the ride to the airport and to see if she received his postcard from Berlin. Here's the message he might leave:

"Hi, Sylvia. I guess you're out. Well, I'm back from Germany, and I want to thank you for the ride to the airport. But what's more important is to thank you for making me think about appreciating what I have in my personal affairs and in my work. I do have some wonderful things going on in my life. I live in a great country; I can easily compare now that I've seen and learned more of Western and Eastern Europe. Our state has superb weather; others are less lucky. I have the right to run my business and travel; others are working hard to have these rights or don't have them at all. And on a final note, I'm shocked that I looked only at what was left undone or missing in my life. You saw the good things that are already there . . . and I am very thankful. Oh, by the way, I've got some German chocolates for you and your fiancé."

SMOOTHING OUT THE BUMPS
POINTS TO REMEMBER/THINGS TO DO

1. Talking too much about the negative side of problems does damage to your efforts.

2. Complaining gives you a reputation as a whiner.

3. Blaming others labels you as negative and even untrustworthy.

4. Focusing on the facts, on what is present, lets you get to the heart of the problem.

5. Problems get solved when they have shape and form.

6. Volunteering for action is a good way to groom yourself to always take responsibility.

7. Be reasonable and moderate as you attempt to change established parts of your life.

8. Remember how much the benefits of productive language outweigh the language of *don't, can't,* and *never.*

9. If you speak in inclusion, the positive results will be enormous.

11

By now you've read a lot about how to stay optimistic and why. Here's where you apply some of the skills and awareness.

HOW TO CHANGE YOUR LANGUAGE

—

*"If thought corrupts language,
language can also corrupt thought."*
George Orwell

In this chapter we will be discussing different categories in which the Language Inclusion Process can be applied. Here's where we will take some time to see just how some of what you have been reading actually fits into real-life situations. Of course, many of you have already made some of these connections and have already applied some of the suggestions to your own personal issues. That's great. It is precisely that type of proactive action that takes new knowledge and plants it into the garden of your life. Here's more information on increasing your harvest. Let's take a look at a few important areas:

- Evaluation
- Appreciation
- Promotion
- Prohibition
- Persuasion
- Motivation

EVALUATION

We, as individuals, are evaluating and making judgments of situations and our experiences all the time. Most of the time, we unknowingly make our evaluations in exclusion. Here are some examples:

- "Not bad."
- "Not too bad."
- "Not as bad as I thought."
- "I don't have a problem with that."
- "I don't see any reason why we couldn't do it."
- "It certainly wouldn't be out of the question."
- "It's not nearly as bad as I thought."

Instead of saying that it "wouldn't be out of the question," you might say, "I certainly would consider it." Instead of saying, "It wasn't as bad as I thought," you might say, "It was actually better than I thought." This change affects your feelings, which affects your thoughts, and, of course, your output in your performance.

This requires practice. And often when you're evaluating anything, you're making judgment calls. The likelihood that you will feel pessimistic about an idea because of your speaking in exclusion is very high. You're much more likely to be optimistic and to move forward when you're speaking in inclusion. So instead of saying, "Not bad," say, "That's good."

Exclusion Examples	Inclusion Examples
Not bad.	That's good.
I can't argue with that.	I'm inclined to agree with that.
I can't complain.	I think it's okay.
I'm not ignoring that.	I'm aware that's a consideration.
It won't hurt.	Here's what will happen.
It's not as bad as it looks.	It's better than it looks.
If nothing gets in our way.	If everything goes as planned.

APPRECIATION

At one of the more successful upscale hotel chains, the Ritz Carlton, employees are trained in very specific language. They are trained to say, "It's a pleasure," instead of saying, "No problem," whenever you show them appreciation. I'm convinced that the Ritz Carlton is perceived as an outstanding hotel chain in part because of the behavior demonstrated by the employees—all of whom say, "It's a pleasure," on a regular basis.

This type of response has to do with how you react when you get appreciation. Suppose someone says to you, "Thanks so much. I really appreciate everything you did." Often you say, "No problem. It was nothing, nothing at all." The reality is this: The first impulse I have when someone says, "No problem," is to say, "Wait a second. You mean there would have been a problem?"

Often, you will try to give appreciation by saying, "I really don't know how to thank you," or "I really don't know how to express my thanks." This can give you the feel of a deficit or inadequacy. "I really don't know how to thank you," could be changed to "It's so difficult for me to figure out a way to properly thank you." In either receiving appreciation or giving it, it is to your advantage to speak in present and positive terms. It does good things for you and for the other person.

PROMOTION

We'll sum up this next category as promotion—the Madison Avenue, advertising kind of promotion. In their ads in magazines, in newspapers, and on television, companies are constantly promoting their products in an exclusionary fashion. But the objective is to:

- Get the market to think about your product.
- Get the market to think favorably about the product.
- Get the market to remember the product.
- Get the market motivated to actually buy the product.

It would be unreasonable to imply that nothing stated in exclusion will ever work. My point is that there may be some extra side effects if we always talk about what is missing. See what you think of these:

- Sara Lee: "Nobody doesn't like Sara Lee."
- Citicorp: "Citicorp, because America wants to succeed, not just survive."
- National Car Rental: "No problem."
- MCI: "If not us, who? If not now, when?"
- Pirelli Tires: "Power is nothing without control."
- Carl's Jr.: "If it doesn't get all over the place, it doesn't belong in your face."
- Paul Mason Wines: "We will sell no wine before its time."
- Vidal Sassoon: "If you don't look good, we don't look good."
- American Express: "Don't leave home without it."

Many of these corporations are quite successful in their industries. The point is to be aware that we are surrounded by various types of language. If we are to keep control of our own optimism, it is best to limit the negative or exclusionary language.

Sometimes it can be the most subtle things that point us in the wrong direction. Most people feel some form of irritation or avoidance when they encounter a bill. At the top right corner of the return envelope is a square in which you are to put a stamp. Very often if you look inside that square, there are printed words, all of which are in exclusion. Those words are: "The post office will not deliver the mail without proper postage." Supposing instead it said, "The post office will deliver this with proper postage." Imagine how our attitude about the postal service would improve.

PROHIBITION

Sometimes it seems that everywhere we turn, we are told not to do something. It's as if we were children again and constantly being watched for our own safety. This reminds me of when I was a young man in my mid-teens. I had recently learned to drive, and on my way home late one night I ran off the side of the road and got into an accident. My mother was quite upset and started to accuse me of doing all the things I was not supposed to do. Believe me, I regularly got into plenty of trouble, but this time I was clean—sober and legal and alone. She gradually calmed down, but the point that sticks with me to this day is the list of things I was prohibited from doing.

Whenever you see a sign posted, it almost always tells you what you are not able to do. Suppose you were to rewrite the signs so they gave their instructions in inclusion as opposed to exclusion. What might they say?

- Instead of saying, "Do not pick the flowers," you could say, "Leave the flowers alone."
- Instead of saying, "No Smoking," you could say, "Smoke Free Area."
- Instead of saying, "No Fishing," you could say, "Fishing Prohibited."
- Instead of saying, "No Swimming," you could say, "Swimming Prohibited."
- Instead of saying, "No Trespassing," you could have some light fun and say, "Trespassers will be eaten," or "If you are here today, you will be found here tomorrow," or even "Is there life after death? Trespass here and find out."
- Instead of "No Littering," you could say "Keep this area clean."

As you go into many coffee shops, a sign in the front window reads: "No Shirts, No Shoes, No Service." Whenever I read "No Shirts, No Shoes, No Service," I start thinking that I'm going to be pretty unwelcome if I'm dressed improperly. The fact that they need to put up the sign makes me wonder who might frequent the establishment, and I assume that they are already prepared to treat me and other customers with contempt if we are dressed wrong. Suppose they were to reword the sign: "You bring the shirt and the shoes, and we'll provide the service." Now that makes me want a hot, steaming cup of coffee.

It's clear to me that we could stand to have a lot more signs telling us what is acceptable or what is unacceptable in a language of inclusion. This creates an entirely different feeling, and a greater likelihood that we would want to obey the recommendation.

PERSUASION

The category of persuasion is one of my favorites because when you really understand how to position your persuasion methods into inclusion, you will have much more horsepower when it comes to persuading people to do things.

In many business and personal relationships, co-workers and partners attempt to persuade each other with some form of "why don't you" or "why don't we."

- "Why don't we get together on Monday?"
- "Why don't you call me on Tuesday?"
- "Why don't we stop doing this?"
- "Why don't we quit getting into fights?"
- "Why don't you get a new job?"

- "Why don't I send that to you?"
- "Why don't I bring the contract over?"

If you and your partner are deciding where to eat and one of you says, "Why don't we go to Rudy's?" the other's first unconscious impulse is to begin to answer the question with "Well, there are three reasons why we don't go to Rudy's: One, I don't want to drive that far; two, I don't really like the food at Rudy's; and three, it's too expensive."

What's interesting is that when you ask somebody, "Why don't we, why don't you?", whether it's in sales or in conflict resolution or any type of relationship situation, the receiver frequently resists you with some form of a "No." However, if you were to change the question from exclusion to inclusion, from "Why don't you—why don't we" to, "How about," or "Let's," the ambivalent person is much more likely to be persuaded.

In our restaurant example, try saying, "Let's go to Rudy's." Your ambivalent partner is much more likely to go along with the idea of Rudy's simply because of the absence of the question that says, "Why don't we?" or "Why don't you?"

Though it can be annoying, one of the ways in which I encourage people around me to become aware of their tendency to use the "Why don't" phrase is to answer the question specifically—if someone says, "Why don't we get together on Monday?", then I might say, "Well, as I think about it, there might be three reasons why we don't get together on Monday." Only after that will they be aware of their tendency to use "Why don't you—why don't we." The sheer change from exclusion to inclusion, from "Why don't we?" to "Let's" or "How about" makes wholesale changes in the way in which the sender feels about the remark and how the receiver accepts it. Here are some additional suggestions:

- Instead of saying, "Why don't we go to Rudy's?", you might say, "How about going to Rudy's?"
- Instead of saying, "Why don't you call me on Monday?", say, "How about calling me on Monday?"
- Instead of saying, "Why don't you get me some coffee?", say, "How about some coffee?"
- Instead of saying, "Why don't you quit smoking?", say, "What are your thoughts about quitting smoking?"
- Instead of saying, "Why don't you quit worrying?", say, "What are your thoughts about learning how to relax?"

What's interesting is you're going to get much more persuasive horsepower when you use "What are your thoughts," "How about," or "Let's" in trying to get other people to sign up to your suggestions.

MOTIVATION

There are hundreds of books and tapes on the market designed to help you become motivated. School teachers, athletic coaches, and business leaders are continually looking for ways to keep their audiences and constituents motivated to do well and perform at higher levels.

Motivation is a mind-state that reflects people's interest in putting energy behind their ideas. Some people are continually motivated; others get urges sporadically, if at all.

Motivation is linked to language. This makes it a very good area in which to apply language skills. Your language can make a huge difference when you want to impact your own motivation or, perhaps, the motivation of those around you.

Some people are motivated by going toward a goal or an objective—they see the benefits. This means that when they decide to take action, buy something, engage the project, or commit their resources, they do so because they are interested in the benefits they will enjoy. They are "going toward" oriented, going toward the pleasure, toward the benefit. They do something in the interest of the payoff they will get.

There are also people who are very "going away" oriented. In making decisions, their motivation is simply to avoid risk and minimize pain. They are reluctant to make quick decisions of any kind. They're always hedging their bets, covering their backsides. They are continually second-guessing, wary of decisions of any kind. Going away from pain is a much more powerful motivator to them than going toward pleasure. If you try to persuade them by explaining the benefits of a course of action, they will almost always resist you because they are interested only in minimizing risk instead of maximizing benefits. These people generally are more afraid and negative. They tend to be more pessimistic in their thinking and probably exclusion-oriented in dialogue.

I believe that most people prefer to think of themselves as "going toward" when it comes to their motivation. However, it's clear that it's very difficult to be a "going toward" person if you're always speaking in the language of "don't, never, and can't."

You might be quite pleased to see how your outlook changes when you speak in inclusion. You might even slowly watch your motivation change from a "going away" perspective to one that goes toward your objectives.

The conclusion is that "going toward" is definitely preferable as a motivator. So to increase this likelihood, speak in terms of "do, always, and can." Then watch the gradual transformation of yourself and those around you from "going away" to "going toward." Your motivation will have a healthier and more powerful feel.

SUMMARY

In this chapter I have presented to you several different categories of applications of the Language Inclusion Process.

- In *evaluation*, I encourage you to say, "Good" instead of "Not bad."
- In *appreciation*, instead of saying, "No problem," I encourage you to say, "It's a pleasure."
- In *promotion*, I encourage you to continually think about what you would like to have happen as opposed to what you would like to prevent.
- In *prohibition*, should you put up signs, have some fun with them and make them more inclusion-oriented.
- In *persuasion*, change from, "Why don't you" to "How about" and "Let's."
- And finally, in *motivation*, concentrate on speaking in inclusion, so that you can gradually change your mind-set of

motivation from "going away" to "going toward."

Each of these will require some practice. As with all new learning, it will seem out-of-place and artificial at first. As you progress, you will become skilled at selecting which battles to fight. I encourage you to avoid becoming fanatical and fearful of every word you plan to utter. But focus on the good stuff, the choices you can make in your words that will lead you to the uplifting results you desire.

SMOOTHING OUT THE BUMPS
POINTS TO REMEMBER/THINGS TO DO

1. Evaluation can be more effective or less effective depending on how you phrase it.

2. Accept acknowledgment and appreciation with a warm and positive reflection of your self-worth.

3. Even good promotional ideas can be improved by stating them in ways that accentuate aspects that are positive and present.

4. Prohibition stifles good and bad activity. It rarely encourages productive initiative.

5. You can maximize the horsepower of your persuasiveness by the way you select your words.

6. Motivation can be toward or away. Useful and productive activity usually springs from going toward pleasurable and beneficial outcomes.

7. Be reasonable in your personal efforts and in correcting others. Stay practical when applying these skills.

8. Search for other applications for the Language Inclusion Process.

12

*Everything isn't always rosy and positive and sweet.
Sometimes you lose and sometimes you must deal with
bad news. Let's see how our journey handles this type
of rough ground.*

DEALING WITH LOSS
& HANDLING BAD NEWS

—

*"I must say to myself that I ruined myself, and
that nobody great or small can be
ruined except by his own hand."*
Oscar Wilde

A friend of mine had just completed a relaxing supper
with friends and family from out of town. They were in
the mountains for the weekend and decided to follow the
meal with a casual stroll under a canopy of stars rarely
seen from cities. As the group walked, my friend silently
hoped that mother nature or some Supreme Being would

see fit to bless them with a shooting star. He had them stop and look up, then walk, then wait again, and so on. He hoped for a dazzling bright one, but it never came. Although he knew there were dozens of shooting stars each evening, he felt there was a lesson to be learned. This lesson was to learn to accept loss or disappointment even when a win was in sight and to know that this will happen again—to be prepared to smile, stay positive, and walk back to the house for a nice, hot, after-dinner coffee. From this mini-disappointment he learned an insightful lesson about being denied what he was expecting and how to handle the mental and emotional feelings.

This chapter is a collection of case studies dealing with loss or handling bad news. I've been telling you to do many things to keep your optimistic attitude. It's also important to give you more ammunition to protect you during the inevitable tough times. Here is a variety of situations where something went wrong or the worst seemed to happen. Is there still room for optimism and a forward-thinking attitude? You bet there is. Let's take a look.

THE MOVIE "JAWS"

Steven Spielberg, in the filming of *Jaws*, said that the mechanical shark kept breaking down. Scenes were cut short or postponed as mechanics hurriedly attempted to repair the vital movie prop. Unfortunately, it continued to have problems. Being on a tight filming schedule, they had to rewrite portions of the script and keep shooting without the shark.

Exclusionary Response: "These lazy support people never get it right. Why is it that whenever we need props and special effects for filming they are never ready. We can't depend on them—they don't come through for us. We'll have to quit filming until we get the shark working properly. If this continues much longer we may never finish this film."

Inclusionary Response: "The mechanical shark will be working again. Since we have yet to know exactly when, we have a few options. We can film other scenes that don't require the shark, or we can rethink some of the scenes and use the suspense and the audience's imagination to get the same scary result. Whatever the case, we'll get it done. We have succeeded before and we will succeed this time."

The Result: The malfunctioning shark forced Spielberg to build in suspense with close-up shots, intrigue, and mystery. The result was a super success that earned great profits, largely as a result of having a broken shark. Most people can vividly recall their reactions many years after viewing the film as they watched the scary scenes in the theater while they held their breath, closed their eyes, or pulled a partner close.

"WIRTSCHAFTSWUNDER"

The Germans called it *Stunde Null* or *Zero Hour*. The Allies had won and the Russians were demolishing Berlin. Hitler was dead in his bunker and payback had begun. The German nation had hit bottom. The Allies divided the country (and also Berlin) into French, British, American, and Russian sectors run by the respective countries. The Germans were required to pay staggering war reparations as punishment for their actions before and during the war. The situation was bleak.

Exclusionary Reaction: "This isn't fair. One political party comes to power and the leader turns out to be a maniac. We never agreed to all that he said or did. It's not our fault. There was nothing we could do to stop him. These war reparations will kill us. How can we recover? There is no way we can rebuild with the entire world on our backs."

Inclusionary Reaction: "There is one direction to go and that is up. We will produce even without our factories. The surviving women will rebuild even without the male population in the cities. The war is over and the mistakes are in the past. Let's focus on peace and progress."

The Result: They called it "*Wirtschaftswunder*," this *industrial miracle* that took place in the ten to fifteen years after World War II. The German people seemed to collectively display the inclusionary reaction that led to quick rebuilding. The investment and the retooling were paying off. Their Gross Domestic Product (GDP) met and surpassed that of most industrialized nations. The German *deutschmark* is now a cornerstone of world financial markets.

HEMINGWAY'S FIRST BOOK

For a writer, the news was bad and would get worse. While living in Paris with his first wife, Hadley, Ernest Hemingway worked diligently on his first book manuscript. It was during the 1920's, and he, a reporter, had decided to write a novel. He and his wife were poor and barely making it on his salary. The book would be their ticket to fame and fortune. Unfortunately, one day he was to meet his wife at a train station and she was to bring him the manuscript, and tragedy struck. There are different versions of what happened, but the result is that the manuscript was lost. At first, a furious Hemingway blamed everyone, including his wife. This was in the days when this mishap meant months of reconstruction, rewriting, and retyping.

Exclusionary Reaction: "It's missing. This is the worst that could ever happen. I will never be able to recreate this work. There is no one I can depend on—not even my wife. It's not fair after all the work I've done. I'll never get the rewards I deserve."

Inclusionary Reaction: "It's missing. This is pretty bad, but there is some hope and there are several options. I have talent and skill. If necessary, I can redo the book and maybe even make it better. I'm sure this has happened to others and they made it through the ordeal. They probably emerged stronger and wiser. So can I."

The Result: Hemingway went on to write and publish blockbusters including *The Sun Also Rises, For Whom The Bell Tolls,* and *The Old Man And The Sea.* He also won the Nobel Prize for literature and is enshrined as an American cultural and literary legend. And the missing manuscript remained missing.

WIN ONE—LOSE EIGHT

A business consultant spent eighteen months developing a proposal and inching through the interview and approval process. She weighed her extensive commitment of time and resources against the nine-part package she hoped to win. The organization was a combined branch of the U.S. government and a major research university. She pressed on and finally received a letter saying that she had won the contract. A few weeks later she was sorely disappointed when she learned that several other consulting firms had also won the contract. Since the clients could not decide in a timely fashion, they opted to divide the contract into pieces and award them to several bidders.

Exclusionary Reaction: "Those sneaky bureaucrats can't be trusted. This isn't fair. Now I've lost several months and significant expense dollars. I also lost eight out of the nine pieces of the contract. I'll never make any money on it at this rate."

Inclusionary Reaction: "This is disappointing but I can handle it. I won one out of the set, and I have already developed most of the materials during the past 18 months. This is a good lesson, so I'll remember to check out the details in the future and keep my expectations in line."

The Result: She faithfully performed the services and refrained from angrily telling the administrators how unfair she initially felt the decision had been. Her program ended up being the only one repeated and the contract was signed again for the next five years.

MISCARRIAGE

A couple decided to round out their family by having a third child. They had discussed, and even argued about, the best timing and how this would impact each of their individual life plans. The first two children were doing well, but the parents agreed that if they were going to do it, they should have a third before too much time had passed. Early in the pregnancy, the doctors noticed complications and warned of the worst. The mother was required to rest in bed for several weeks in an attempt to hold off labor long enough for the fetus to develop to survival stage. It failed and the couple lost the baby.

Exclusionary Reaction: "We never should have tried this. There are already too many children in the world. We shouldn't have more than two. It will never work out. It's too late. We're getting too old to have another kid. How would we have time to take care of the new baby? We probably wouldn't have the patience anyway."

Inclusionary Reaction: "This is a heartbreak, but we do have two wonderful kids. This happens to a lot of couples and most of them get over it. The complications can be avoided, and with some luck our next try will be successful. These feelings of depression and anger are normal and will probably go away—soon, we hope and trust."

The Result: The couple did continue to try. It took a while to recover from the miscarriage and to sort out their emotions. Within two years, the mother gave birth to a healthy baby girl. The delivery had some complications but everything worked out fine. The age difference between the children is perfectly acceptable, and the addition to the family has greatly enriched their lives.

BRAIN TUMOR

Joanna's boyfriend was dying of a brain tumor. It had started with seizures and other episodes that hinted that something was wrong. Luis and Joanna loved each other and had planned to eventually marry. The seizures got worse, and Luis lost his driving license and later his job. The first surgery removed as much of the tumor as possible. A second brain surgery in three days was needed to remove a blood clot. The remission lasted about 18 months, so they set a wedding date. Unfortunately, just after invitations were mailed, Joanna called everyone to say that the doctors had found several new tumors in the x-rays and that Luis only had about two months to live. After many tears and much reflection, the wedding was canceled.

Exclusionary Reaction: "I can't see how I'll make it through this. This never should have happened to us. There is no other man that I love. I'll never be able to replace him. My life is missing all the things most people deserve to have."

Inclusionary Reaction: "It's difficult to see any good in this. I don't know what good I might find, but I'll keep trying to make sense of this. It hurts, and many other people feel the hurt with me. I'll begin to consider how I'll cope now and in the future. When he's gone, it will take some time to recover and feel that my life is worthwhile again."

The Result: When Luis passed away, Joanna felt the pain of his loss, along with the relief that his suffering had ended. She changed her working hours from night shift to day shift and gradually began to make new friends. She took up skiing, scuba diving, and in-line skating. These activities helped her stay mentally and physically healthy while she dealt with her loneliness and hurt.

SUMMARY

Dealing with bad news requires an ability to position the trauma in a way that helps you to recover. The Language Inclusion Process will enable you to recover faster. Times can be tough and situations can be heartbreaking. We are humans and we come equipped with a wonderful range of senses and emotions. We may not always understand the meaning or the reasons attached to losing or why we must experience the bad things in life. What we do know is that certain reactions can make losing even worse and the bad news more tragic. The best response is to use what we can control (our language) and focus on rebounding from the losses and recovering from the bad news with our heads held high and our optimism fully nourished.

SMOOTHING OUT THE BUMPS
POINTS TO REMEMBER/THINGS TO DO

1. Your reaction to small losses or disappointments is a clue to how you may react to larger issues.

2. Explore feelings of loss or disappointment. It helps to briefly think about them or talk with someone about them.

3. An optimistic explanatory style interprets difficult events in terms of possibilities and options.

4. A pessimistic explanatory style describes setbacks with limits, problems, and deficits.

5. Inclusionary language gears you to consider tangible and realistic ways you can deal with work and life.

6. Exclusionary language can take heartbreaking situations and make them worse. Inclusionary language is the better choice.

7. The Language Inclusion Process will help you turn personal loss or tragedy into potential-packed options.

8. Sometimes you lose and sometimes the news is bad, but your reaction is the critical element.

13

"Rewards are seldom on time" are the words from a person's story told in this chapter. You can win in your struggle to stay optimistic by understanding the nature of paying your dues.

PAYING YOUR DUES

——

A successful business owner spent 15 years starting and building a consulting business. He provided a combination of seminar training and published materials for his clients. He had the usual setbacks, but the thing that always made him bristle was when friends and family, seeing that he was truly struggling, would ask, "How long are you going to keep trying this?" He disliked the question because up until then he never thought about giving up or caving in. He was passionate about the vision he saw and the structure he was putting into place to carry it out. The question "How long are you going to keep trying this?" planted a suspicion about his skills and doubts about his perseverance. He loved his family and friends, but he feared what this question would do to him and his business.

During my years as a therapist, and most recently as a consultant and author, I have been able to observe many different reactions to stress, fear, and self-doubt. What I have noticed is that the man or woman who tackles the mental side of the challenge will most likely win out. What I mean is that a person has a choice to simply work harder on his or her tasks (I'll call them "house cleaning" items) or to spend his or her creative energies on the "home building" challenges. The former activities only make the present situation look a little better, but the latter move the person mentally and emotionally to a higher level of understanding and readiness.

The healthiest people I've seen in my practice or in my consulting and training activities are the ones who recognize the danger of comments and behaviors that start sapping their mental edge or their emotional power. It's as if someone whispered into their ears, "You are going to fail. You are going to fail," over and over again. This deadly seed, once planted, will take root and, if watered and fertilized, will keep growing and growing. In a large part, this is the message of this book. Those seeds come from every direction, including from within ourselves. The smart thing to do is to manage the negative sources that we can control. We have little control over what other people say or do. We certainly have little control over what or how the media portrays deadly events and commonplace occurrences. We do, however, control what we say about things and how we interpret them.

BACK TO OUR STORY

We left our business owner tangled up in a difficult mental and emotional situation a couple of paragraphs ago. What's a good way to protect his mental edge and his emotional power? In his case, he developed a quick answer (and practiced it) so that when some good-hearted person asked about the length of his entrepreneurial patience, he could quickly respond, "As long as it takes—I may be doing this until the day I die." He recalls two things happening after he started using this statement. First, people never again asked him how long he could endure the beginning struggles of a new business. They stopped implying that quitting was an option. Somehow, his actions and statements delivered the message. Second, it gave him a rush of adrenaline and a powerful mental and emotional boost. The words he said to himself and to others had an instant effect on the way he felt. And it felt good, so he used it often and reaped the benefits.

Our business owner came away from the above experience with not only a successful enterprise but also with a little saying to remind himself to be patient: "Rewards are seldom on time." It helps to determine what reward you can reasonably expect at any period of time. Instead of always looking at the final payoff, it helps to learn about the intermediate stages of successful accomplishment. There are rewards at each stage based on the level of dues you have paid.

PAYING YOUR DUES

Our work at the JM Perry Corporation often involves taking a group of individuals through structured exercises designed to teach them the increased leverage power of working as a unified team. We include trust exercises, risk-taking simulations, "icebreaker" events, and multi-tasking coordination challenges. One of the good outcomes occurs when one member of the group comes to realize that working together makes almost any task easier and more likely to succeed. We are thrilled when we hear this. We even have a name for it—reframing. We've all taken a cherished photograph and decided to buy a new frame for it. We remove it from the old frame and insert it into the shiny new one. The same picture in a new frame adds a bright spot to the room. Your eyes notice that something has changed. So you might say reframing is when you take an old way of looking at a concept and surround it in new understanding and insight.

"Paying your dues" may sound negative. You may even think it fits poorly into this book on finding a direction toward optimism. How about if we reframe that sentiment? The world is tough. Our challenges can seem overwhelming. This chapter is meant to explore a heavy-hitting tool that takes into account the real and tangible issues of this world (and your personal situation). It's hard to manage a career and a personal life. Let's reframe this "difficulty" into something we can grow from and grow with. What can we say about paying our dues? Some of the following phrases make those dues sound less negative and a little more useful:

- Investing our dues.
- Paving the way.
- Creating our place.
- Deserving our success.

A useful way to look at paying dues is to compare it to the price we pay for a delicious and memorable meal. Or how about the dollars you pay to go see a movie that strikes you at the core and keeps you thinking about the plot for days and weeks to come? One more example: Raising and educating children can be viewed as a wonderful experience or a lifestyle disturbance and a financial nightmare (similar to how individual performers look at the first stages of team-building). Some of our political leaders, local planners, and fellow voters view the sacrifices required to raise and educate children as far too unpalatable—they think it is not worth the time and money. The rising wave of disaffected teenagers and lawbreaking juveniles testifies to this unresolved problem. Enlightened politicians, planners, and voters look ahead and envision healthy human beings who are well-exposed to the basics of education along with the variety of cultures and ways of thinking. This is a powerful payback—a new generation capable of digesting tough issues and implementing solutions to current and future human challenges. That's reframing the topic of paying our dues.

There are three levels of dues, tolls, or charges— *survival* dues, *advancement* dues, *legacy* dues—that may explain some of the complex parts of your life. You may wonder why you work so hard but others seem to do better than you. You probably get tired and feel that you deserve good things to happen because you are so tired. Your fatigue can mistakenly be interpreted as your passport to rewards. Unfortunately, fatigue has little to do with the dues you have paid. It often only relates to your attitude surrounding a project or your level of expectation. These three levels of dues will assist you in calibrating your expectations about when you can reasonably count on the good things coming back to you. If you do not calibrate, you may be in for some frustrating periods in your life. We may think our rewards are too late, when in fact, they tend to track—with some delay— the level of dues we have paid. See what you think.

SURVIVAL DUES

This is that first stage that everyone must experience. You can call this the initiation that all must endure and master if there is to be any more progress in whatever field the person has chosen. Survival dues allow you to continue your existence in your particular field or endeavor. They rarely allow you to grow or to prosper significantly. These are the kind of trials and tribulations discussed at the water cooler, over a beer, and at reunions.

Survival dues are rarely avoided; they are endured the first time around, and, to the novice, they are mistaken for a magical ticket to lifetime rewards and satisfaction. Some well-intentioned folks think that since they paid these dues and did the basics, they should get anything they want and that they deserve to protest or complain when someone says or implies that these dues are not enough. Once in a while a herd mentality takes hold and some people, rather than progressing to a higher level of performance (and the dues that accompany it), criticize, stockpile, and prepare for the worst. Sometimes they even create the worst—but of course, they rarely feel the fault is with themselves because they firmly believe they have paid their dues and deserve better.

The truth is that these survival dues are far from paying the requisite debt to get what they think they deserve. Sure, you get some rewards after paying these survival dues but they are neither exceptional nor lasting. They only get you into the balcony for the play, or the bleachers in center field for the game, and you'd better bring your binoculars.

Survival dues:

- High school graduation.

- Basic sports awareness training.
- Public speaking essentials.
- Average discipline in eating.
- Reading anything.

ADVANCEMENT DUES

For those who want to keep rolling, they soon find that their rewards are delayed while they again pay their respects to the god of dues. Advancement dues are those that must be paid to separate yourself or your efforts from the masses. The masses did the survival stuff and are sitting around waiting for the sweepstakes van to drive up and deliver their big check. Paying this next level of dues is an acknowledgment that the sweepstakes van is not going to come and you are unlikely to win the lottery, but if you do it will be icing on your cake because you refuse to sit around and be inactive.

The delay between paying these dues and your rewards is longer than in the earlier category. For some reason, the universe seems to test your patience to see if you really deserve to be placed in this advancement category.

When the good stuff arrives, it's quite pleasant, but one minor glitch begins to show up—others become jealous and accuse you of getting something you don't deserve or of being a non-conformist. Some groups put heavy ethnic pressure on the person to try to rein them back into the pack. This is often why so few will progress beyond this category. For those who venture out, the sacrifice of paying advancement dues is often the first hurdle, and then a second hurdle is that their nonperforming peers stigmatize them in hurtful ways. Advancement dues produce substantial rewards that surpass those that come with survival dues. At the advancement level, you sit in the center section for the play or along one of the baselines at the ball game.

Advancement dues:

- College graduation.
- Basic sports team training.
- Public speaking essentials skills.
- Moderate discipline in eating.
- Personal growth reading.
- Diverse affiliations and partnerships.

LEGACY DUES

This opportunity is only recognized by the seasoned veteran, the investor with keen eyes and a complete sense of self-accountability and self-responsibility. These folks take the responsibility and dole out the credit. They see through the transparent veils of race, entitlement, victim-hood, and "silver spoons." They know that what they get is exactly what they've earned and that's all. These results at the legacy level seem to take forever, but since getting there is assured, the journey is fantastic. The mental attitude and eternal optimism are profound. These people inspire awe in others. They are charming without trying to charm. They are benevolent when it is needed regardless of the spotlight. They know that the loop is completed through relationships, so they pay whatever the cost to develop and groom sterling partnerships built on trust and unwavering integrity. Legacy dues rarely seem like dues at all. The folks in this category have used their language choices, their emotions, and their thought processes to construct a firmly positive and optimistic personality. It is effortless. They already went through that. Sometimes they yelled and screamed and wondered why rewards took so long, but that was in the past—now they know. They are now sitting up front soaking up the performers' expressions and interpretations, and they also get to chat with the ball players as they enter and exit the dugout directly in front of their seats.

Legacy dues:

- Advanced studies.
- Multi-dimensional physical skills.
- Mastery in public speaking.
- Superb discipline in eating.
- Personal growth and "classics" reading.
- Decades-long planning and collaboration.

MENTAL EDGE

Over the years I have seen quite a variety of people who have lost their mental edge in major areas of their lives. Sometimes I see the results in their personal relationships and other times my staff and I see it in their corporate enterprises when we take them through skill-building trainings, leadership coaching, or team-building events. They often lose it in the heat of the battle; in other words, they wilt like a seedling in the hot sun. Others have never developed this mental edge and the seedling never even sprouted.

"As long as it takes" was a phrase used toward the beginning of this chapter. The person using it was responding to questions about his perseverance in a new venture. This response is one example of taking control of your mental edge. You can start by being clear on the direction you want to take and the type of dues you must pay. Your mental edge is boosted or hindered by the seeds you allow into your life. Your language can stop some of those negative seeds from ever hitting the ground. And for those that slip by, your word selections—your language of inclusion—can minimize the impact of those seeds that challenge your healthy optimism.

EMOTIONAL POWER

"Rewards are seldom on time" is another phrase we have explored in this chapter. Far from being negative or pessimistic, for you and me to acknowledge that rewards take time is a way to match our expectations to the real dues we have chosen to pay. Emotions are difficult to control. It takes some advance planning and doing your homework to groom your emotional power.

SUMMARY

Instead of remaining in the dark, we can become aware of how rewards are actually earned. Survival requires that we pay survival dues. We get what we pay for and that's all. If advancement is our aim, we must calibrate ourselves to pay additional dues to earn the goodies in this second category. If our aim is to leave a lasting legacy, we have entered the third level of requirements. This is a long-term, slow-brewing process. It would be foolish to expect legacy-type rewards after only paying the piper for the first two levels of dues. You will fail unless you develop the mental edge and emotional power that comes from firmly aligning your expectations with the efforts required to get the results you want and ultimately will deserve. Therefore, the message here is that learning to speak with the Language Inclusion Process will require time and paying your dues, and with enough practice, you will see great results.

SMOOTHING OUT THE BUMPS
POINTS TO REMEMBER/THINGS TO DO

1. Remember the saying "Rewards are seldom on time."

2. Be careful of spending too much time on "house cleaning" activities at the expense of "home building" behaviors.

3. In most endeavors you need to pay your survival dues first.

4. Just when you think you've made it, it's time to pay your advancement dues.

5. Of course, you can stop at this point, but to make a lasting impact you are required to pay your legacy dues.

6. After dues are paid you get wonderful value for your time, energy, and money.

7. Your mental edge is sharpened by carefully guarding which seeds you allow into your life.

8. Your emotional power gets stronger when your expectations match the dues you choose to pay.

9. The Language Inclusion Process is the method for making those dues much more bearable.

The Final Word on Optimism

Here is a gentle attempt at reframing something familiar to all. This take on the Ten Commandments pulls together what we have been exploring throughout our journey on the road to optimism.

EPILOGUE

THE NEW TEN COMMANDMENTS

—

It's a stormy, dark night. I'm in bed thinking that I must be dreaming. In the distance, an older man who looks very much like Charlton Heston with a mane of black and white streaked hair appears wearing a white robe and a red cape and sandals on his feet. He's coming down the mountain, and he's got these two huge tablets in his hands. As he approaches, I can make out his face clearly, and the objects in his hands appear to be heavy and big. Thunder crashes and lightning explodes behind him. The man steadies himself and begins to read from the inscriptions on the tablets:

ONE
Thou shalt have no other gods before me.

TWO
Thou shalt not make unto thee any graven image.

THREE
Thou shalt not take the name of the Lord,
thy God, in vain.

FOUR
Remember the Sabbath Day to keep it holy.

FIVE
Honor thy father and thy mother.

SIX
Thou shalt not kill.

SEVEN
Thou shalt not commit adultery.

EIGHT
Thou shalt not steal.

NINE
Thou shalt not bear false witness against thy neighbor.

TEN
Thou shalt not covet thy neighbor's wife.

It's Moses reading the Ten Commandments, and I'm thinking to myself, "What am I doing here on Mount Sinai? And furthermore, why am I having the Ten Commandments read to me?" I'm starting to feel a little afraid, a little shameful, and definitely guilty.

Suddenly I start thinking to myself, "What's going on here? What's God trying to tell me? Why should I feel so afraid, shameful, and guilty?"

At this point my alarm clock wakes me up. I hear, "You're listening to KNBR!" Wow, what a strange dream! Boy, am I glad to wake up, because I sure want to quit feeling so shameful and guilty.

So I get out of bed to shower, shave, and brush my teeth. It's time for my morning routine so that I can be presentable for another day's work. My ritual begins by turning on the television. Oops, you remember what happened earlier—the negative anchor people, the upset weatherman, the horrendous traffic report. This is too much! Isn't there another way to start this day?

I return to dreamland. It's still dark and it's still stormy, so let's replay the scenario and this time let's change the language.

Moses is once again descending from Mount Sinai, and he really does look like Charlton Heston. My sense of wonder and great expectation fills the air as he reaches the plateau just above my head. Moses commands attention! Charlton Heston certainly plays Moses with great power and verve.

He's about to impart the laws that will become the best known principles on the planet for thousands of years to come. This time, however, the Ten Commandments sound a bit different. This time they are uplifting. Instead of proclaiming the usual "Thou shalt nots," this time in my dream, Moses, with a sense of enormous pride, awe, fascination, and command—including a giant smile on his face—reads a new version!

ONE
Worship only me as thy God.

TWO
Hold thy God above all else.

THREE
Honor the name of the Lord, thy God.

FOUR
Keep the Sabbath Day holy.

FIVE
Honor thy mother and thy father.

SIX
Honor and preserve life.

SEVEN
Be true to thy spouse.

EIGHT
Respect the property of others and leave it be.

NINE
Be honest and demonstrate integrity.

TEN
Be appreciative of thine own spouse and content with
what you have.

It is interesting, that some conspicuous words are
absent in this scene—"kill, adultery, steal, bear false
witness, and covet." Moreover, these commandments
leave me with a decidedly better feeling—more hopeful,
positive, and more optimistic. There is a better likelihood
to be loving and forgiving. Now, rather than knowing

what "not to do," I'm more confident in my dream of what "to do."

The alarm goes off and the radio is tuned to a local station. I wake up, get out of bed, clean myself up, and get dressed. I detour to the television to start my morning ritual of listening to those bright, shiny faces telling me about the world.

In this version I hear the anchorwoman say, "The President said today in his address to Congress, 'This is reprehensible behavior, and we are going to hold this blustering dictator accountable.'" It sounds as though the President is on top of the situation, and I'm feeling rather confident.

After contemplating the President's determined and spirited speech, I listen to the weather report. "It looks like it's going to be another gorgeous week. The temperature is just about right, the mid 70's; in fact, it looks as if this great weather pattern is here to stay for a while." The weatherman with more of the report: "The pollen count is very low today, so it will be a great day for the noses of all you allergy sufferers." Now that's great news, because it appears that I will be highly unlikely to have any hay fever attacks today.

Well, my day is getting better by the minute. These news people are really on a roll. I'm feeling pretty confident and I'm bordering on happy. I head to the kitchen for some coffee. While still listening to the television, I hear them start the traffic report. The traffic reporter looks very happy and excited as he says, "Great news to report to the commuters this morning. The roads are clear and it's smooth sailing for anyone heading into town. You'll be able to get to work on time today."

The traffic reporter is actually pleased and happy for a change. Well, what do you know!

It affects me, too. This is truly a remarkable day. I can get to work on time and am free of any accidents I would need to avoid.

Then the financial reporter comes on the television and says, "Mortgage rates are predicted to remain constant for the near future. Trading on Wall Street is brisk. Good news for all of you potential home buyers out there; the average price of a home is expected to remain about the same for the next year."

What I've learned in my first waking hour is that the Ten Commandments are encouraging and powerful and make me feel inspired. I've also learned that a lot of things are happening. A foreign dictator's behavior needs to be improved, and we are going to do something about it. The weather is great. The traffic is clear. Pollen is low. Wall Street is steady. The price of homes is remaining constant. So I think to myself, "Well, Mitchell, you can be happy if you want to because things look pretty good."

I head to the front door to retrieve the newspaper to see if it's filled with as much of "what is happening" in the world news as the television. And what do you know! In my version it is!

I drink my coffee, grab my briefcase, and head to work. It is clear sailing, as predicted. With so little traffic, I get to work on schedule.

I meet Bob in the elevator. "How's it going, Bob?"

"Great!"

In the hallway I run into Lou. "Hey, Lou, what's going on?" I ask.

"Things are going pretty well, and I'm pretty happy."

I enter my office and ask, "Good morning, Stacy, has it been busy?"

"Things are pretty quiet this morning, Dr. Perry. You had a few calls last night, but it looks as though you're free to do whatever you'd like this morning."

I head to my desk, scan the few messages I had from last night, sit down, and contemplate how I feel so far about my day. Well, I feel wonderful. I feel great. I feel encouraged. I feel optimistic and ready for the day.

This is what I call a preferable reality. As you can see from this version of a usually negative story, language has an immense impact on our behavior and the way we think and feel. Unfortunately, the story most of us experience is a bit different.

What adults mostly focus on is *what is not*. Think about how you might feel about the Ten Commandments if they were interpreted in terms of what is, what we are supposed to do, as opposed to what we're not supposed to do. Notice how it's entirely possible we might feel a lot less guilt and shame and a lot more love and forgiveness.

My greatest hope is to see what would happen if, from the Ten Commandments to the weather report, we could experience life most of the time on an inclusion basis. It's enriching to see how your perspective on reality influences the nature of your behavior and how by simply changing your language, you can change your life!

APPENDIX

30 WAYS TO IMPROVE YOUR OPTIMISM

—

1. Read about optimistic people to find what challenges they dealt with and how they kept it all together. Their stories will pull you through some tough times.

2. Seek out optimistic people and make an effort to learn about them and do things with them. These folks are usually open and warm as long as you respect their time.

3. Speak in inclusion. Talk about what is there, what is real, what is present in any situation. It may seem awkward but it will get more comfortable as time goes on.

4. Watch for feedback from others as you change your language. Notice the positive effect it will have on them if you do not overdo it during the awkward stage.

5. Pay attention to how children naturally speak. See if you can spot their inclusionary language choices and how they come off as optimistic in what they say and do.

6. Assume you are an optimistic person. Say things, do things, and think things that build on this assumption that you are already optimistic (see next four items).

7. Build habits that lock the positive into your life. Focus improvement efforts on the television, news, and shows that you watch to minimize the anger and hostility that is broadcast and to keep your attitude strong and optimistic.

8. Build habits that lock the positive into your life. Focus on all that you read. Simply avoid the negative, hate-filled content.

9. Build habits that lock the positive into your life. Focus on your friends and family. Do the thumbs-up test. Starting with a thumb up, estimate where your family and friends take you. Does the thumb stay up, turn sideways, or turn thumbs-down?

10. Build habits that lock the positive into your life. Focus on words you say to yourself and others. Think and reframe before you speak.

11. Change the subject when friends and family dwell on the angry or negative side of things. Offer other topics or open unexplored areas of the original subject—there's got to be something positive to say.

12. When you must vent your occasional negative feelings and emotions, take a breath and mention some portion of the situation where you are favored or blessed.

13. Ask for feedback early on so that constructive or even negative criticism doesn't shock you and cause you to lose ground. This can be a part of your mental preparation for performance in personal areas or on the job.

14. Explain the good things that happen to you as if you are fully deserving of having them happen to you. Take a breath of air and feel the good emotions that go with getting the things you deserve (after paying your dues).

15. Explain the bad things that happen as part of what happens on the way to success. They happen, but it doesn't mean you are undeserving or unworthy or being unjustly punished—just smile, breathe, and go on.

16. Take the high road when explaining things that are puzzling or unclear. Give the positive possibilities the benefit of the doubt. At least start your attitude and assessment of a situation on a positive and optimistic track.

17. Cut others some slack. Until they prove otherwise, assign good and wholesome motives to other people. Assume they are good and reliable and competent.

18. Take some action to delve into the issue or situation. It doesn't matter what—just do something. It will make you breathe easier and even relax your shoulders a bit.

19. Write down a few sentences or a paragraph describing a scene or situation that is putting pressure on your good attitude. Record facts, your impressions, and your feelings.

20. Make a drawing or an illustration. This is even better if you are *not* an artist. Use stick figures or lines to sketch what you feel is happening.

21. Prepare in advance. Put the pressure on yourself to practice, gather materials, or whatever it takes to be ready to confront or handle a situation.

22. Think ahead. Use your commute time, on-hold time, or in-line time to think about your next plans or future steps you can take. Don't let this mental planning build anxiety; let it build your plan for coping with possibly unpleasant or challenging events and staying very optimistic.

23. Stop yourself mid-sentence if you are on the way to a negative or exclusionary statement. Pause and complete

the phrase or thought in a way that leads to useful feelings and thoughts.

24. Use the Start/Stop Principle. It's easier to start a productive activity than to stop a nonproductive one. Use your calendar or bulletin board to schedule the things you can do to keep optimistic.

25. Change your scenery. However you do it, a shift in your usual patterns will lead to a fresh and energetic outlook on your work and your life. Go somewhere different, do something unusual.

26. Plan your day, your week, and your month. This short-term schedule helps you to avoid trouble spots in advance.

27. Build time into your schedule for diversions such as walking, hobbies, reading, and even getting regular meals. All this supports your productive attitude.

28. Build some personal phrases or sentences you can say to yourself that support your confidence and your competence.

29. Hang around children and young people. They're not so scary! A lot of the optimism they have will rub off. If you find some going through dark, negative periods, support them but remember: That, too, will rub off.

30. Talk with older folks about the good times and what advice they might have for you. You'll brighten their day. And this will brighten your day.